INCLUDES
1 CD–ROM

D0126525

35

The
VECTOR BRUSH
SOURCEBOOK

For more excellent books and resources for designers,
visit www.howdesign.com.

14 13 12 11 10   5 4 3 2 1

Distributed in Canada by Fraser Direct
100 Armstrong Avenue
Georgetown, Ontario, Canada L7G 5S4
Tel: (905) 877-4411

Library of Congress Cataloging-in-Publication Data

ISBN: 978-1-4403-0301-2

Layout by Emily Portnoi
Art Director Tony Seddon

fw
media

The VECTOR BRUSH SOURCEBOOK

300 unique brushes for digital illustration

Emily Portnoi

Additional material collated
by Luke Herriott

HOW BOOKS
Cincinnati, Ohio
www.howdesign.com

Contents

About this book

This book and its accompanying CD aim to teach you everything you need to know about Illustrator brushes— how to make them, apply them, edit them, and use them to stunning effect. It may at first seem that they are just one limited function of a large illustration package, but the array of effects they can achieve is vast.

There are other types of digital brushes, which work with bitmaps and bitmap software such as Adobe Photoshop, but we're focusing on Illustrator brushes because of the flexible nature of vector illustration. Unlike bitmaps, vectors don't use pixels, so aren't dependent on screen resolution. This means they can be changed after their creation, and changed as many times as you like; they don't have to be erased or retouched. Their size can also be increased and decreased infinitely, without any loss of quality. All of which makes vectors perfect for illustrations, because they are precise, editable, and create smaller file sizes.

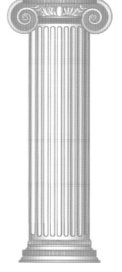
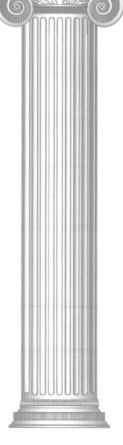

Content

The main body of this book is divided into four sections, one for each type of Illustrator brush: Calligraphic, Scatter, Art, and Pattern.

Each brush section includes:

- An explanation of how to make that brush type
- Details of the setting variants
- Fully-illustrated tutorials
- A directory of the original brushes on the accompanying CD with explanations of how they were created
- A gallery of images showing the vast array of styles and effects that can be achieved through the use of brushes

The final section in the book is Tips and tricks, which will answer any questions that have not already been covered.

The shortcuts used throughout the book are for Mac users, but there is a chart of shortcuts for both Mac and PC at the back of the Tips and tricks section.

CD

The accompanying CD is compatible with both Macs and PCs, and works with all versions of Illustrator, from Illustrator 10 and onwards. It includes 300 original brushes, which are copyright free, and are at your disposal to use as you wish. All the brushes are saved as EPS Illustrator files, which can be opened as Illustrator documents displaying the brushes, or from within other Illustrator documents as Brush Libraries.

The brushes are organized by brush type and all the files are named according to the page the brush or brushes appear on in the book. Some brushes have their own Illustrator page and library, and others are grouped in families.

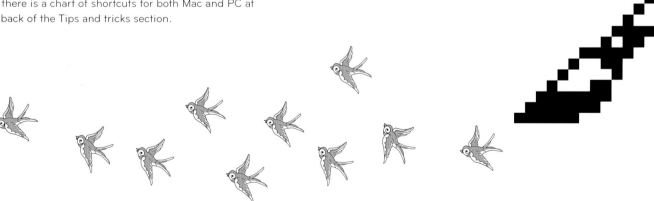

What are Illustrator brushes?

Illustrator brushes are stylized brush strokes that can be applied to a path in the vector illustration package, Adobe Illustrator. Because these brushes are made using vectors rather than bitmaps, they are incredibly flexible. They can take on almost any form, can always be adjusted, and scaled up or down to whatever size you want.

Making paths

Vector images are made up of lines and anchor points. The anchor points control the length, shape, and curve of the lines. Each anchor point has two control handles that determine the arc of the line as it enters and exits the anchor point, allowing you to make and control curves.

Applying brushes

Once you've drawn your path, you'll want to give it some style. Maybe you'd like it to look like a charcoal drawing, a piece of lace, a flock of seagulls, or footprints in the snow—the options are endless. All you have to do is create and apply the right brush.

Brushes are accessed from the dedicated brushes palette, and are categorized into four different types: Calligraphic, Scatter, Art, and Pattern. Illustrator comes with a selection of preset brushes, but by the time you've finished reading this book, you'll be able to create your own unique brushes.

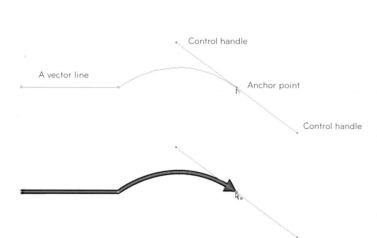

Control handle

A vector line

Anchor point

Control handle

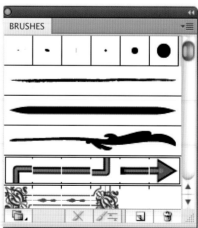

What can they be used for?

Due to their adaptable nature, brushes can be used for everything from decorative borders on CVs and business cards to complex illustrations.

Once you've created a brush, you can use it as often as you like. Meaning that, for a little work up front, you can save yourself a lot of time later on and produce images that look like they've taken a lifetime to create.

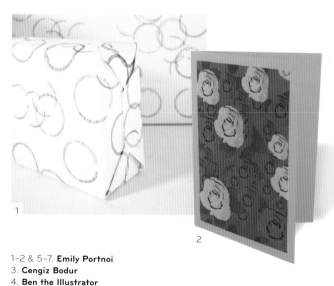

1-2 & 5-7. **Emily Portnoi**
3. **Cengiz Bodur**
4. **Ben the Illustrator**

The four types of brush

Calligraphic brushes resemble a calligraphic brush or pen. You can adjust their size, angle, and pressure. Calligraphic brushes are the only type of brush that can be used with the Blob Brush tool, a new feature of CS4, and they work especially well with a graphics pen and tablet.

Scatter brushes are a single object scattered along a path. You can adjust how the objects scatter from the path, how far they scatter from each other, and how much they vary in size and angle.

Art brushes stretch a single object along a path. You can affect their scale, how they proportionate themselves to the path, and the direction they travel along the path.

Pattern brushes are by far the most complex as they are made up of five different tiles—Side, Outer Corners, Inner Corners, End, and Start—which each fit onto the path in the specific places. The Side tiles, which tend to make up the majority of the path, will repeat to fill the path, so unlike art brushes, the brush detail doesn't become stretched.

Calligraphic brush

Scatter brush

Art brush

Pattern brush

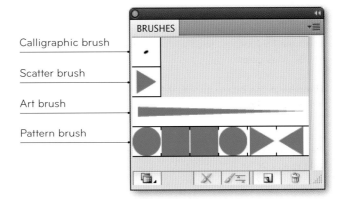

Where are they hiding?

All four types of brush can be found in the Brushes palette in Illustrator. To view this palette choose Window > Brushes, or hit the F5 function key, which also displays (or hides) the Brushes palette.

The palette can be moved around the screen or can sit in the horizontal panel dock on the right of the screen.

In CS4 and CS5 you can also find the Brushes palette in the application bar at the top of the screen. This drop-down palette sits to the right of the Stroke palette, and is exactly the same as the loose palette.

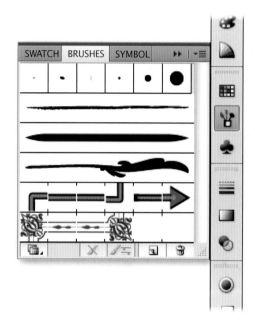

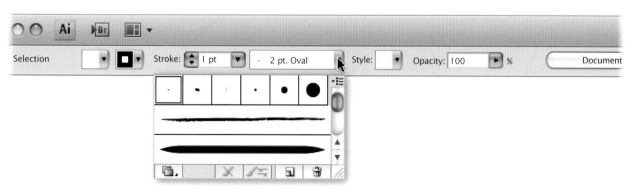

Features of the Brushes palette

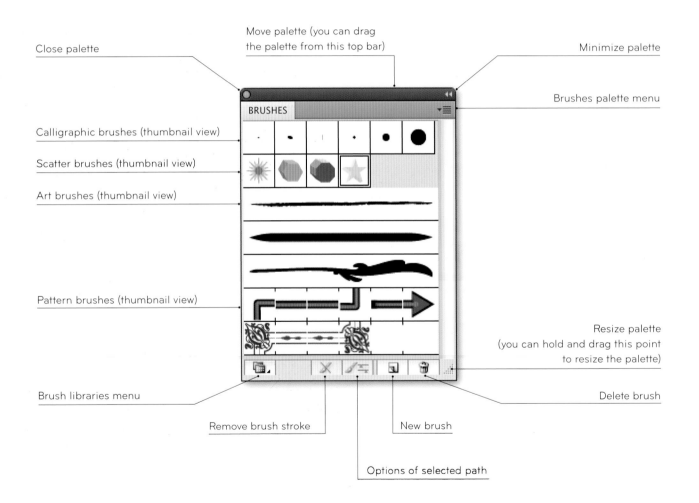

Close palette

Move palette (you can drag
the palette from this top bar)

Minimize palette

Brushes palette menu

Calligraphic brushes (thumbnail view)

Scatter brushes (thumbnail view)

Art brushes (thumbnail view)

Pattern brushes (thumbnail view)

Resize palette
(you can hold and drag this point
to resize the palette)

Brush libraries menu

Delete brush

Remove brush stroke

New brush

Options of selected path

Functions of the Brushes palette

The Brushes palette not only shows you which brushes you can use, it also allows you to add, delete, duplicate, adjust, and save them too. And, as with many Adobe products, there is more than one way to do every task.

Viewing brushes

The brushes sit in the palette grouped by type: Calligraphic, Scatter, Art, and Pattern.

In the top right-hand corner of the Brushes palette there is a fly-out menu where you can select which of the four types of brush to display by clicking on or off the brush type. You can also choose between displaying brushes in List View or Thumbnail View. Thumbnail View gives you a bigger picture of the brush, but List View tells you the name of each brush and includes an icon representing which type of brush it is.

You can rearrange the brushes in your palette simply by dragging them up or down to a new position. However, they will only rearrange within their own type, so a Scatter brush can't be put in the middle of the Pattern brushes.

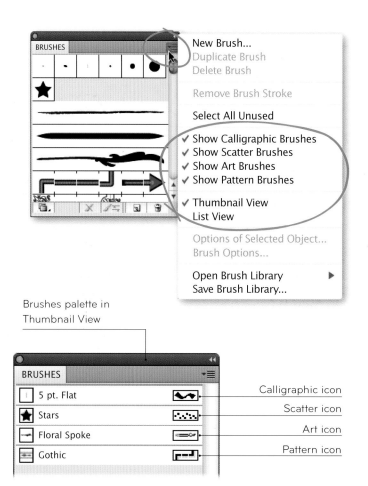

Brushes palette in Thumbnail View

Calligraphic icon
Scatter icon
Art icon
Pattern icon

Adding brushes

You can add brushes to the Brushes palette by opening a Brush Library: Brushes palette menu > Open Brush Library; or Window > Open Brush Library; or click the Brush Library menu icon in the bottom right-hand corner of the palette). New Brush libraries will open in their own palette. Click on any brush you want from the Brush Library, and it will load into your main Brushes palette; from here you can use it whenever you want (and it will stay there, even if you close the brush library it came from).

To move a brush from one document to another, select any path with that brush applied to it, and then copy (⌘ + C) and paste (⌘ + V) it into your new document. You can then delete the path with the brush applied, and the brush will still remain in the Brushes palette of your new document.

You can also add your own brushes—just click the New Brush icon at the bottom of the palette or select New Brush from the palette menu. Alternatively, drag and drop artwork that you want to make into a brush into the Brushes palette, (Calligraphic brushes are an exception to this; because they are always a circle or ellipse, they can only be made by clicking on New Brush from the drop-down menu or on the New Brush icon). All of these routes will bring up a dialog box asking you which type of brush you want to make.

For more detailed information on how to create each type of brush, see the "explained" section of each brush chapter.

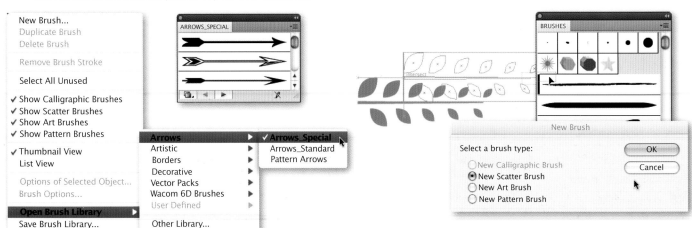

Deleting brushes

To delete a brush, simply select a brush or brushes, then scroll down the palette menu to Delete Brush or click on the trash can icon at the bottom of the palette.

There is also an option to Delete All Unused Brushes from your palette, which gets rid of any brush that isn't applied to a path. This can be a good way of tidying up your palette after lots of experimentation. It is worth remembering that storing lots of brushes in your Brushes palette can really increase your file size, so it's best to strip out the ones you're not using.

Saving brushes

There are two ways of saving brushes. The first is in the Illustrator file they were created/used in; the Brushes palette will remember which brushes you have loaded and which you have deleted, so each file can have a different set of brushes in its palette.

The second way to save brushes is in a Brush Library. A library can be one or more brushes, you can save it anywhere, and open it from within an open Illustrator document. Just select the brushes you want from your Brushes palette, then scroll down the palette menu to Save Brush Library, or click on the library icon. Then name the library and save it.

To open these created libraries, choose Open Brush Library from the menu and then click on Other Library, or choose Other Library from the library icon fly-out menu. If you want your newly created Brush Library to appear in the Brush Library menu, make sure you save it in the brush folder of your Illustrator file.

Documents with brushes in their Brushes palette can also be opened as Brush Libraries, as is the case with the EPS files on the CD accompanying this book.

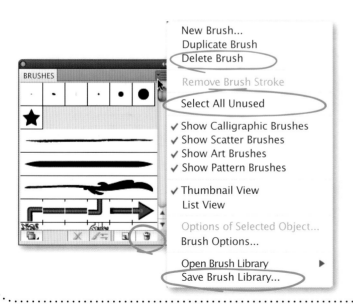

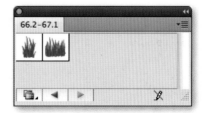

Each brush type has its own Options window. (The options within the window vary for the four different brush types, and are explained in their relevant chapters.) You set the option for a brush when you first create it, but the Options window can always be accessed, and the option changed at any time.

Editing brushes

To edit a brush, double-click on that brush in the Brushes palette (you cannot edit brushes from within Brush Library palettes, only your main Brushes palette). This will bring up that brush's Options window.

Once you're happy with the adjustments you've made, click OK, and the Brush Change Alert window will appear. Click Apply to Strokes if you want all the existing strokes applied with that brush to be updated. Click Leave Strokes if you want existing paths to remain the same and a new brush to be created that incorporates the changes you've made.

Editing a specific path

To edit the brush options for a specific path, you must first select the path you wish to edit, then click on the Options of the Selected Object icon at the bottom of the Brushes palette. You can edit more than one path at the same time, so long as the paths have the same brush applied (with the exception of Calligraphic brushes, where different brushes can be edited simultaneously).

The Stroke Options windows for each type of brush includes almost all of the same features found in their Brush Options window. The only difference is that you cannot change the brush name for any of the brush types, you can't change the direction of an Art brush, and you can't change the tiles of a Pattern brush.

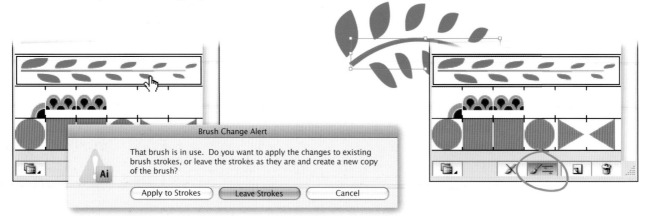

Duplicating a brush

To create a duplicate brush choose Duplicate Brush from the fly-out menu and change the settings if you choose.

Alternatively, if you adjust the options for a brush that is already applied to a path on your page, you can choose to Leave Strokes when the Brush Change Alert window appears. This means your original brush will remain and a new one, with your amended settings, will also be created.

Removing brush strokes

You can also remove a brush stroke from one or more paths by selecting the path and then clicking the Remove Brush Stroke icon.

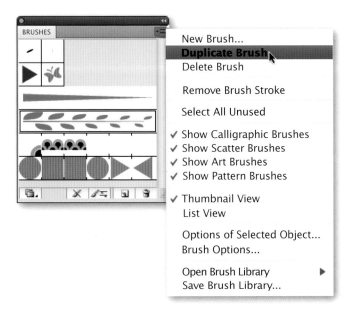

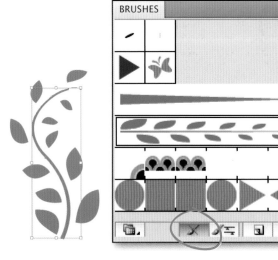

Resizing brushes

Each of the four brush types has scale and proportion options, which you set in the Options windows. These options can also be edited for individual strokes by selecting the paths you wish to adjust and then clicking on the Selected Object icon at the bottom of the Brushes palette.

However, you can also adjust the scale of your strokes through the stroke weight setting, or by resizing the stroke the brush is applied to.

Stroke weight

Changing the stroke width from 1pt to 2pt has the same effect as doubling the diameter of a Calligraphic brush, doubling the width of an Art brush, or doubling the scale of a Pattern brush.

The only brush which reacts differently is the Scatter brush. When you increase the size of a Scatter brush in its Brush Options, the objects will enlarge and the space between them will adjust accordingly. But when you increase the stroke width of a path with a Scatter brush applied to it, the objects increase in size, but the space between them will stay the same.

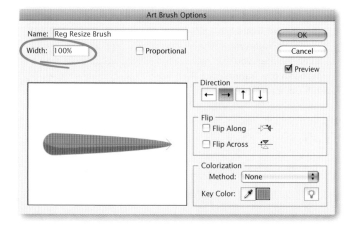

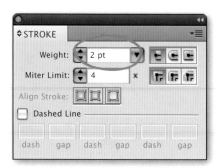

Resizing strokes

If you have Scale Stroke & Effects checked in Illustrator's General Preferences, the size of a brush stoke will also change when you enlarge or shrink the path it is on—either through the Transform palette, or by dragging the handles of the object's bounding box.

Resized Scatter brush examples

100% Scale
with 1pt Stroke Weight
on original size path

200% Size
with 1pt Stroke Weight

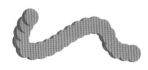

100% Size
with 1pt Stroke Weight

100% Scale
with 1pt Stroke Weight
on scaled-up path

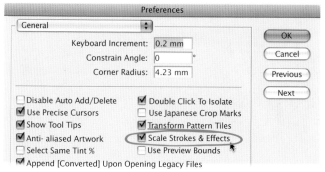

Colorization

Colorization is the one Options window feature common to Scatter, Art, and Pattern brushes (for details about coloring Calligraphic brush strokes see page 33).

The Colorization method of a brush, along with the stroke color in your Color palette, dictates which colors your Scatter, Art, or Pattern brush will draw in. To change the Colorization method, select one of the following options in the Brush Options window:

None keeps a brush the same colors as the original artwork, which is displayed in the brushes panel.

Tints makes the brush draw in tints of the stroke color. Any parts of the brush that are black will become the stroke color, any parts that aren't black become tints of the stroke color, and white parts remain white.

The Tints setting works best with brushes that are originally black and white or shades of gray, as these will produce the most accurate tints of your stroke color.

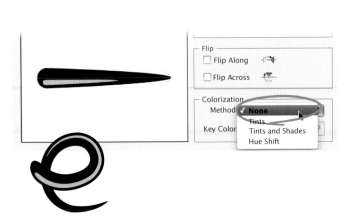

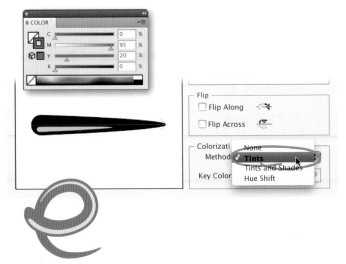

Tints and Shades ensures that any black and white in the original brush will remain black and white, and everything in between (color or gray) will become a tint of the stroke color.

Hue Shift identifies the key color in the brush artwork and displays it in the Key Color box. Everything in the brush artwork which is the key color becomes the stroke color, and all other colors become a blend of their original color and the stroke color.

By default, the key color is the most prominent color in the brush, but you can change the key color by clicking on the Eyedropper tool and then on your chosen color on the brush displayed in the Options window.

Examples of the difference between each Colorization method are shown in the Colorization Tips window, which you can bring up by clicking the light bulb icon.

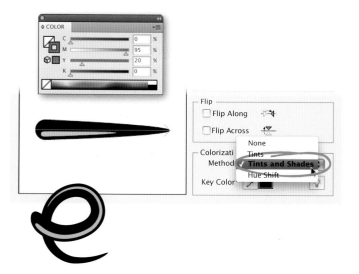

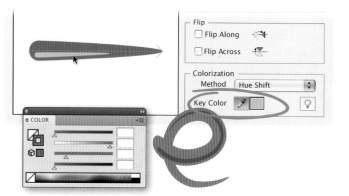

Application

Brushes can be applied to paths in two ways:

1. Select the Brush, Blob Brush (only available in CS4), or Pencil tool, then select which brush you want, and start drawing.

If you use the Paint Brush or Pencil tool, you can still select the path after it's drawn and change the brush which is applied to it. However, if you use the Blob Brush tool, your brush will already be converted to outlines, so cannot be changed.

2. Draw a line or shape, select it, and then choose the brush you want to apply to it.

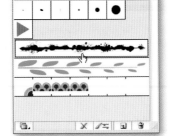

1. Drawing in a Calligraphic brush

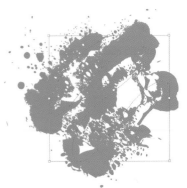

2. Applying an Art brush to a path

Path drawing tools

Since you can apply a brush retrospectively to any path you've drawn, you can use any of the drawing tools: Pen, Line (and any of the Line tools), Paintbrush, or Pencil. However, drawing with the Paintbrush or Pencil tool gives more options for working with brushes. (The Blob Brush also has advanced options, but only works with Calligraphic brushes, see page 34 for details.)

The Paintbrush tool draws paths and shapes. If you have a brush selected as you draw, the brush will automatically be applied to that path. You can draw with any brush you like, or apply any brush to a path after it's drawn. The Paintbrush tool will apply any sensitivity settings which are assigned to a brush (Calligraphic and Scatter only), and when drawing with a Calligraphic brush, the Paintbrush tool applies the selected brush stroke to a path as you draw.

The Pencil tool can have any brush applied to a path it has drawn, but won't actually draw with a brush. It also doesn't use the pressure sensitivity setting of a brush.

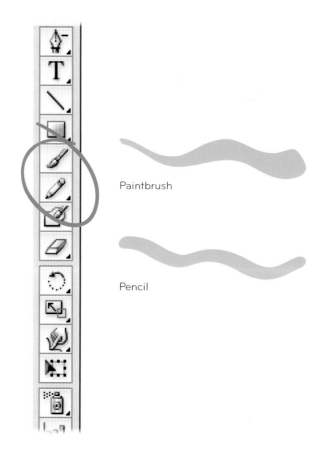

Paintbrush

Pencil

Path drawing tool options

Double-click the Paintbrush or Pencil tool icon (or press return once you have selected either tool) and you'll bring up their Options windows. Here you can adjust how the tool draws.

Tolerances

These sliders affect the look of your path. You may find that you are drawing away quite happily, but the second you release the mouse, the path you've just drawn seems to lose its shape; this is because you have the wrong tolerances.

Fidelity controls how many anchor points are placed on the path that you are drawing. The higher the Fidelity value, the less anchor points on your path, and the lower the Fidelity value, the more anchor points, making the path more precise and adaptable.

Smoothness affects how much Illustrator smooths out your path. The higher percentage you put your slider on, the more Illustrator will smooth your path.

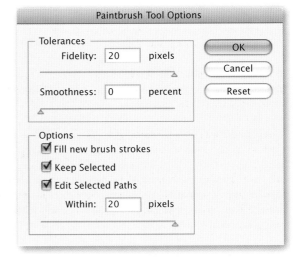

High Fidelity   Low Fidelity   High Smoothness   Low Smoothness

Options

These check boxes affect what happens to your path
once you have finished drawing it.

Fill new brush/pencil strokes lets you choose to have your
path automatically filled or not, so long as you have a fill color
selected in your Color palette.

Keep Selected lets you choose whether or not you want your
path to remain selected after you've finished drawing it. If
you're just drawing one thing and then editing it straightaway,
it's best to have Keep Selected checked. But if you want to
draw a number of paths at one time, then it's frustrating to
have to keep deselecting the path you've just drawn before
you can draw the next.

Within pixels is either the most frustrating or the most
useful option, depending on how you like to draw. You may
have noticed that when you draw a new path near an existing
one, they morph together. This slider determines how close
your new path must be to an existing one before they will
join. The lower the slider, the closer your two paths can be
without joining. However, the paths can't merge at all if the
existing path isn't selected, so if you're not a fan of this
feature, it's best just to turn off Keep Selected.

Calligraphic brushes

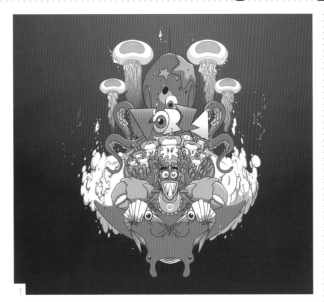

1. **Forza illustration by André SMATIK Ljosaj**
This image was used on a flyer and T-shirt for the musician Daniel Bortz. All the lines were dawn with a 1.5pt, pressure-sensitive Calligraphic brush.

2. **Colorbees on a Swarm illustration by André SMATIK Ljosaj**
The lines in this illustration were created with a 1.5pt, pressure-sensitive Calligraphic brush.

3. **Portrait by Emily Portnoi**
This illustration was entirely created with the Blob Brush tool, a variety of different pressure-sensitive Calligraphic brushes, and a graphics pen and tablet.

4. **Calligraphy by Emily Portnoi**
Traditional calligraphic writing created with a graphics pen and tablet and Calligraphic brushes.

5. **Letter Cake typographic illustration by Josh Scruggs**
Experimental alphabet created using a Wacom tablet and a pressure-sensitive Calligraphic brush to create an extreme thick/thin contrast.

6. **Zebra illustration by Emily Portnoi**
Pressure-sensitive Calligraphic brushes with a high variation were perfect for creating this zebra's stripes.

Calligraphic brushes explained

Calligraphy is the art of producing beautiful, stylized handwriting. Calligraphic vector brushes simulate a calligraphy pen or brush, so they can be used to create some really stunning type and wonderful illustrations. Plus, you can always go back and adjust what you've done without ever spilling a drop of ink.

Calligraphic brushes have some of the most sensitive settings of the four brush types, allowing you to fine-tune your brush to a high degree. When working with a graphics pen and tablet, the pressure and angle sensitivity settings let you create a brush that responds just as a real calligraphy pen would. They are the only brush type that can be used with the Blob Brush tool, and they are also the only brush type that will appear on the path as you draw when using either the Paintbrush or Blob Brush tool.

Making a new Calligraphic brush

Calligraphic brushes can only be ellipses (like a real pen nib), so you can't make a new Calligraphic brush by dragging a shape into the Brushes palette, as you can with other brush types.

To make a new Calligraphic brush you must either:

1. **Choose New Brush** from the Brushes palette menu.

2. **Click on the New Brush icon** at the bottom of the palette.

Both of these actions will open the New Brush window. Select New Calligraphic Brush, click OK, and the Calligraphic Brush Options window will open.

1.

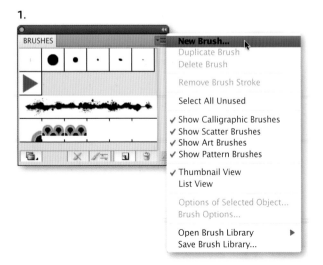

2.

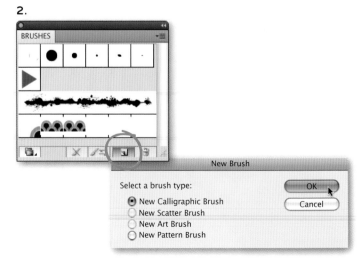

Calligraphic Brush Options

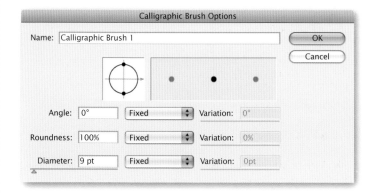

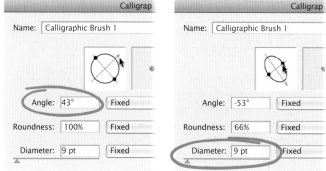

From the Calligraphic Brush Options window you can adjust and preview your brush's Angle, Roundness, and Diameter.

Angle affects the angle of your brush.

Roundness sets the shape of the brush and can range from 100% round (a circle) to 0% round (completely flat).

Diameter determines how large the brush will be at its widest point.

There are two ways of adjusting the Angle and Diameter options—you can manipulate the brush diagram or manually enter a percentage in the relevant panel.

When using the diagram, move the arrow head to affect the Angle, and the two opposite black dots to affect Roundness.

Option menu variants

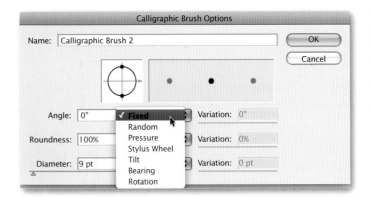

When using Random with Angle, you can set the slider to anywhere from 0° variation of the original angle, to 180° variation. 0° is the angle set for that option, and 180° is 180° clockwise from the angle set for the option.

When using Random with Roundness or Diameter, the figure you enter for these options sets the middle/norm, and the slider sets the variation from that figure. For example, if you set the Diameter to 15pt and the variation value to 0pt, the brush will always have a 15pt diameter, because there would be no variation. But if you changed the variation value to 10pt, the brush could vary 10 points either way from 15pt, so it could be anything from 5 to 25pt wide.

As with Scatter and Art brushes, each option has its own menu in the form of a drop-down list, which lets you control variations within that option. The panel to the left of the diagram previews what your brush will look like. It shows three images of your brush, so you can see the variation within your settings.

Fixed is the default setting, and means that the brush will have a set angle, shape, or size.

Random creates a brush that will change angle, shape, or size from one stroke to the next. However, it will only vary from the value you have set that option to, and within the range that you specify by moving the slider on the right.

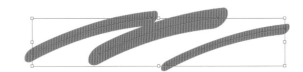

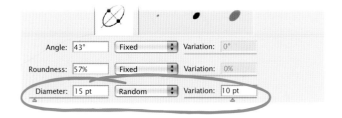

Sensitivity menu variants

The Pressure, Stylus Wheel, Tilt, Bearing, and Rotation menu variants are common to Calligraphic and Scatter brushes, and are specifically for use with a graphics pen and tablet. Unlike Fixed or Random, they only work when you draw with the Paintbrush or Blob Brush tool.

If you don't have a graphics pen and tablet, none of these variants will work for you. You can still see them and set them, but when you draw, your brush will consistently be the maximum value the variants could produce. For example, if you set the Diameter to 15pt and the variation value to 10pt, the brush will always paint with a 25pt diameter.

If you do have a graphics pen and tablet, it does not necessarily mean that all the sensitivity variants will work for you, because not all tablets can detect Tilt, Bearing, or Rotation. Pressure is the most widely supported feature, but it depends on the model and make of pen you are using.

You can adjust your graphics pen's sensitivity, with the Tip feel slider in the Pen Tablet window in the System Preferences. The softer the tip feel, the wider the range of pressure available to you in Illustrator.

The menu options

All the option variants do the same thing—they vary the Angle, Diameter, or Roundness of your brush as you draw, so that a brush can change on a single stroke. The variant you choose depends on which method you prefer.

Pressure creates a brush where the Angle, Diameter, or Roundness vary depending on the pressure you apply when drawing your path with your pen. How sensitive your pen and tablet are to pressure will depend on the make and model and its settings. This sensitivity is measured in levels and not all pens have a high enough sensitivity level to detect subtlety of pressure.

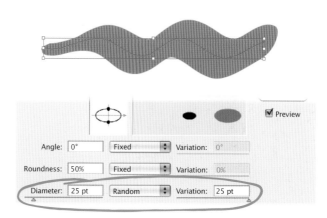

Stylus Wheel can only be used if you have a pen with a stylus wheel; these are found on airbrush pens. The stylus wheel on these pens controls the virtual ink flow, simulating an airbrush rather than a pen.

The Stylus Wheel setting means that the Angle, Diameter, or Roundness will vary depending on the position of the wheel on your pen as you draw.

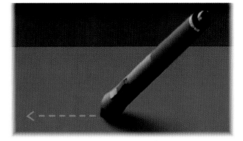

Bearing varies the brush depending on where the tip of the brush is pointing.

Tilt varies the brush depending on the angle of your pen to the tablet.

Rotation varies the brush stroke depending on how the pen is rotated around the axes of the pen itself.

Preview and coloring

See what you'll get

The comparison preview panel will show you the variations of your brush, but in addition to that, there is the preview function. As with all Brush Options windows, checking the Preview box means that the changes you make in the Options window will preview on any existing strokes with that brush applied.

The best way to get the right settings for your Calligraphic brush is to draw a test stroke with either the Paintbrush tool (even if it's just a scribble), and then bring up the Options window and adjust the settings while having the Preview function checked. This way you will see the effects of the changes on your test stroke.

Once you're happy with the way your test stroke looks, click OK. The Brush Change Alert window will then appear; click Apply to Strokes.

Coloring Calligraphic brush strokes

Calligraphic brushes are the only type of brush not to have Colorization options; this is because no Calligraphic brush will have any original color or color variation. To change the color of your Calligraphic brush strokes, simply change the stroke color in your Color palette.

You can choose your color before you draw or afterward, and you can change it as many times as you like.

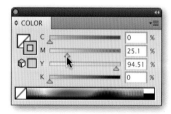

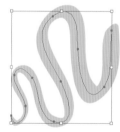

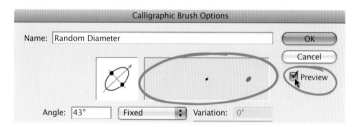

The Blob Brush

The Blob Brush is a brand new feature to CS4 and can only be used with Calligraphic brushes or its own default brush. You select it by clicking on the Blob Brush icon, just below the Pencil tool icon in the tools palette, or by using the shortcut shift + B.

You paint with the Blob Brush exactly as you would with the Paintbrush tool, but rather than giving you a path, it produces a filled shape with no outline. You can then adjust that shape as you would any other: you can change the color, add effects, manipulate the anchor points, edit or erase it with the Eraser tool, and even apply a brush to its path. This means that you can paint in a more natural way, building shapes up, rubbing them out, and painting over them.

Coloring with the Blob Brush tool

The way that the Blob Brush colors is slightly confusing, but very relevant if you want to merge shapes. Because the Blob Brush is still a brush tool, it paints with the stroke color. But because it creates a shape rather than a path, when you finish painting you'll see that the stroke color becomes the fill color for that shape.

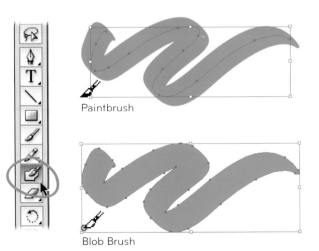

Paintbrush

Blob Brush

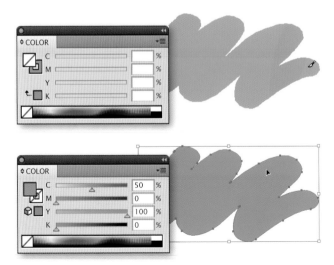

Merging shapes with the Blob Brush tool

The Blob Brush can merge shapes as you paint. Any new shape you paint will merge with existing shapes, so long as they share the same fill and stroke color, they overlap, and there are no other shapes in between.

So if you want two shapes to merge, your new shape must have the same stroke color as the fill color of your existing shape or shapes. If you haven't changed colors since painting the objects you want to merge with, then this will automatically be the case. However, if you have been changing colors, you can guarantee this by having the existing shape or shapes selected as you paint over them. This ensures that your newly created shape shares the same attributes as the ones you selected, and will therefore definitely merge.

The Blob Brush can merge as many objects as you like, so long as you paint over all the objects you want to merge. It can also merge with shapes not created with the Blob Brush, as long as they have the same fill color and no stroke.

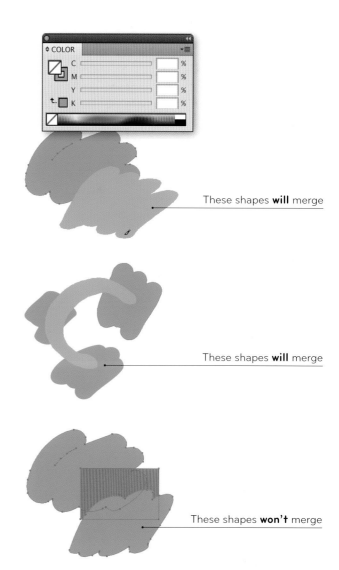

These shapes **will** merge

These shapes **will** merge

These shapes **won't** merge

Stealing attributes

The Blob Brush's trick of stealing an existing shape's attributes can be very handy, even if you don't want your shapes to merge.

The new shape you paint with the Blob Brush can take on the style attributes of any shape selected as you paint, as long as New Art Has Basic Appearance is *not* checked in the Attributes palette menu. Outlines and gradients won't copy, but fills, drop shadows, transparency, and pattern fills can all be copied.

Choosing a Blob Brush

The Blob Brush will paint in whichever Calligraphic brush is selected. If no brush is selected or a non-Calligraphic brush is selected, the Blob Brush will use its default brush setting. You can adjust the default brush settings in the Blob Brush's Options window, or you can change the size of the brush using the bracket keys; pressing the left bracket key ([) while using the Blob Brush tool will make the brush smaller, and the right bracket key (]) will make it bigger.

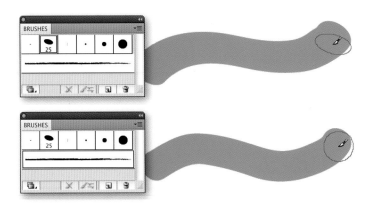

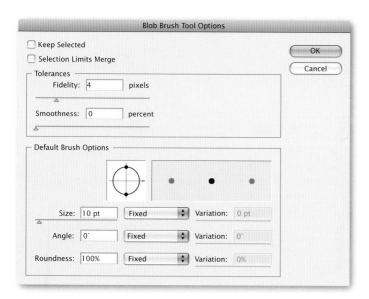

Blob Brush Options

Like the Paintbrush tool the Blob Brush has its own Options window, with many of the same features. To access this, double-click on the Blob Brush tool in the Tools palette, or press return once you have selected the tool.

Keep Selected lets you choose whether or not you want your shape to be selected after you've finished painting it. This means it will remain selected as you continue to draw and will therefore automatically merge with the next shape you draw if they overlap.

Selection Limits Merge lets you choose whether or not you want new shapes to merge only with selected ones. But, if you have this option checked, but no shapes selected, the Blob Brush will merge with any matching shape, as long as you paint over it.

Tolerances

The Tolerances sliders work in exactly the same way as they do for the regular Paintbrush tool.

Fidelity controls how closely your path follows what you draw by determining how many anchor points are placed on your path. The higher the Fidelity value, the less anchor points and the looser your path, and the lower the Fidelity value, the more anchor points and the more precise your path.

Smoothness affects how much Illustrator smooths out your path. The higher the percentage you put your slider on, the smoother your path.

Default Brush Options

These options are exactly the same as those for the Calligraphic brush. They control the Size, Angle, and Roundness.

Illustrative 1

Because of this brush's Fixed 134° Angle it has a similar width on the horizontal and vertical strokes.

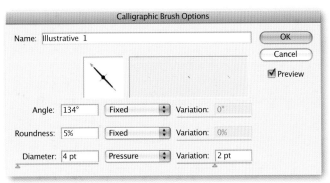

Illustrative 2

Because this brush is almost vertical it produces great variation between horizontal and vertical strokes.

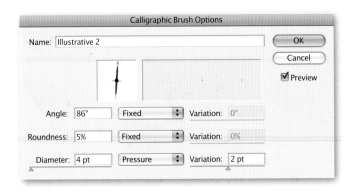

Illustrative 3

This brush is completely horizontal, due to its 0° Fixed Angle, so as with Illustrative 2, it produces great variation between horizontal and vertical strokes.

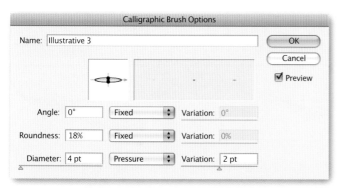

Ribbon Wedge

A Calligraphic brush can be the best way to illustrate a ribbon, especially if you want the ribbon to have movement.

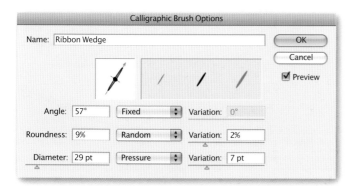

Leaf Wedge

Because of its 49° Angle this brush can make beautiful leaf shapes with simple strokes.

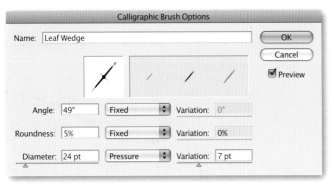

Thick Wedge

This chunky wedge brush will grow or shrink in size depending on how much pressure you apply when drawing with it. If you don't have a graphics pen and tablet, change the Diameter menu to either Fixed or Random.

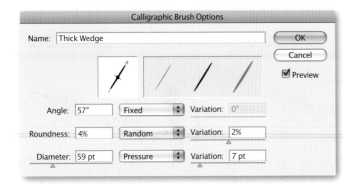

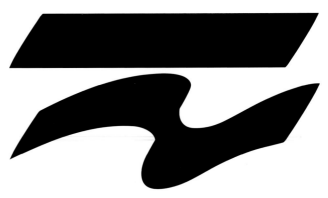

Quill 1

These brushes are great for creating elaborate lettering with thin
horizontal strokes and thick vertical strokes.

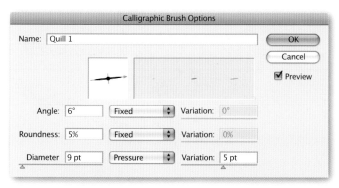

Quill 2

Because the Diameter option is set to 15pt Pressure variation, it is capable of producing
strokes which vary from 2pt to 32pt.

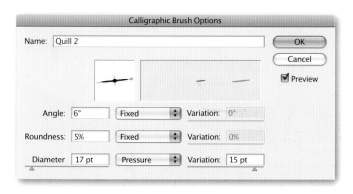

Quill 3

This small and narrow brush is good for the fine detail on your lettering.

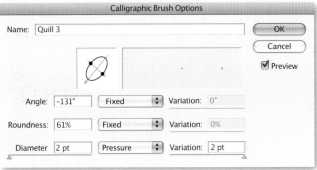

All Fixed

With all its Options menus set to Fixed, this is a good, reliable brush.

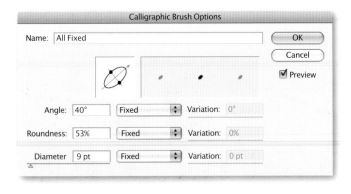

Diameter Pressure

This brush is great fun for messing around with the pressure sensitivity of your graphics pen and tablet.
A featherlight touch will produce a 2pt nib, but with a heavy hand it will increase up to 22pt.

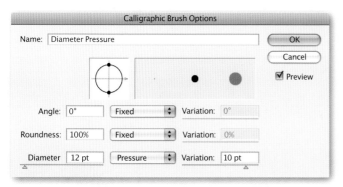

Roundness Pressure

The Roundness menu option for this brush is set to Pressure with 40% variation, so
it is perfect for showing the difference pressure can make to your strokes.

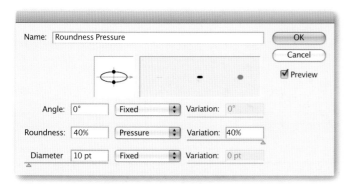

Tilt Angle

This brush's Angle menu is set to Tilt, which is the angle your graphics pen is at to your tablet.

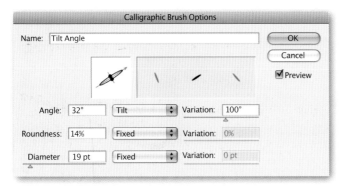

Flat Outline 3pt

This brush gives great variation between horizontal and vertical strokes because of its near horizontal angle.

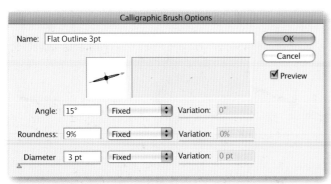

Design: André SMATIK Ljosaj

Flat Outline 5pt

This brush gives great variation between horizontal and vertical strokes because of its vertical angle.

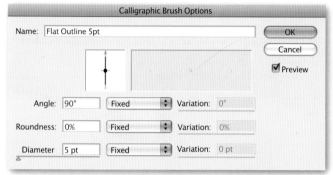

Design: André SMATIK Ljosaj

Round Outline 3pt

This fixed option brush gives a consistent stroke.

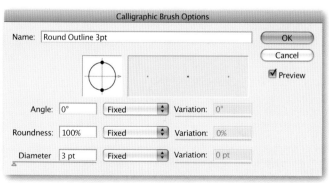

Design: André SMATIK Ljosaj

Round Outline 7pt

This brush has a fixed Diameter of 7pt, but you can still affect its width by changing the stroke weight of the path it is applied to.

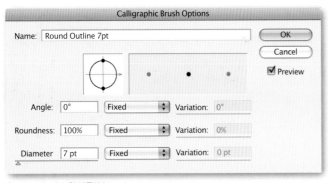

Design: André SMATIK Ljosaj

Oval Outline 2pt

These brushes were used in the creation of the Forza illustration on page 26.

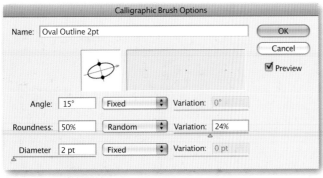

Design: André SMATIK Ljosaj

Oval Outline 5pt

The Random Roundness option for this brush, and the 40% variation, means that it can be anything from 10% to 90% round.

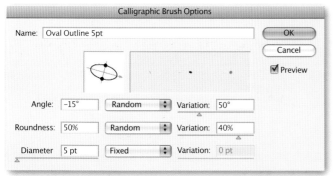

Design: André SMATIK Ljosaj

Pressure Round Outline 1pt

The Pressure setting for this brush's Diameter means that a light pressure will result in a 0pt stroke and heavy pressure will produce a 2pt stroke.

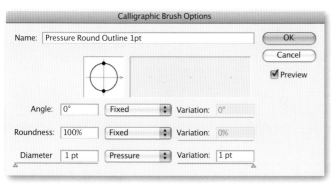

Design: André SMATIK Ljosaj

Pressure Round Outline 1.5pt

These Pressure Calligraphic brushes were used in the creation of the Forza illustration on page 26.

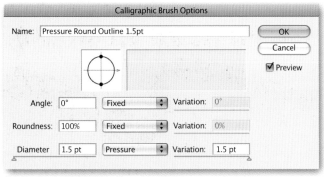

Design: André SMATIK Ljosaj

Zebra Angle 75

All the following Zebra Calligraphic brushes were used in the creation of the Zebra illustration on page 27.

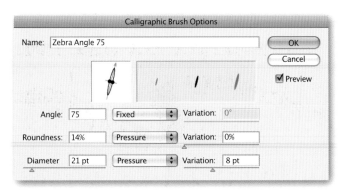

Zebra Angle 122

Because of the fixed 122° angle of this brush, you will only notice the shallow roundness of the brush when it is applied to a wavy or curved path.

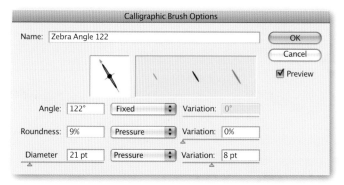

Zebra Angle 153

The Comparison Preview panel in a Calligraphic Brush Options window shows the variants your setting will produce in your brush.

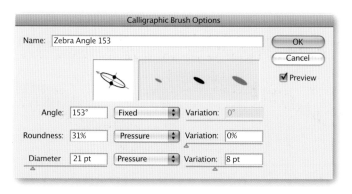

Zebra Diameter 21

Because the Diameter option for this brush is set to 21pt and the variation is set to 8pt, the lightest touch of your graphics pen will produce a 13pt stroke, and the heaviest touch will produce a 29pt stroke.

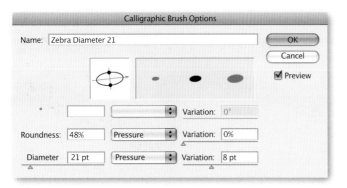

Zebra Roundness 22

This brush has its Roundness set to 22% with maximum variation, so a stroke could be anything from 1% to 44% round, as is shown in the Comparison Preview panel.

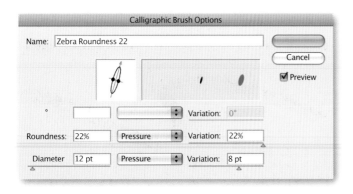

Zebra Roundness 40

All the Calligraphic brushes featured in this book and on the accompanying DVD have the Preview box checked, so you can always see how existing strokes will be affected.

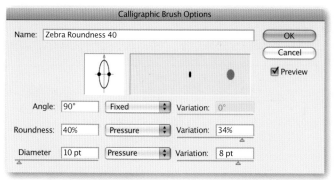

Zebra Roundness 53

You can use Calligraphic brushes that have sensitivity settings even if you don't have a graphics pen and tablet, but you won't get the variations of Angle, Roundness, or Diameter.

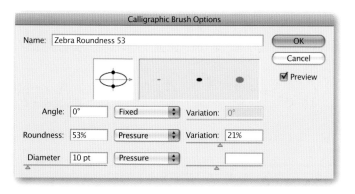

Scatter brushes

5

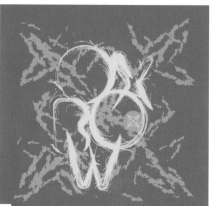

6

7

1. **Kumoku animation by Weirdink**
The bubbles in this animation were created with an original Scatter brush, the tentacles and hair were made with an Art brush.

2. **Bracelet illustration by Emily Portnoi**
This simple illustration was created using the Pressure Pearls Scatter brush, with a graphics pen and tablet.

3. **Follow Your Dreams illustration by Ilias Sounas**
Original Scatter brushes were used to roughly place shapes in this illustration, which were later expanded and their positions adjusted.

4. **Starlings illustration by Emily Portnoi**
The effect of a flock of birds was produced by combining the three Starlings in Flight Scatter brushes over a photograph,

5. **Exterior design by André Nossek**
The Worms Scatter brush featured in this exterior design proposal for the Watergate Club in Berlin was specifically created for the task.

6. **Oxbow T-shirt by André Nossek**
This T-shirt motif, for surfwear brand Oxbow's 2010 collection, was created using only Art and Scatter brushes.

7. **Gift wrap by Emily Portnoi**
The floral paper was created with the Rose Head 2 and Rose Leaf Scatter brushes, and the coffee-ring paper was made by combining the three Coffee Ring Scatter brushes.

Scatter brushes explained

Scatter brushes use one image and scatter it along a path. Unlike Art and Pattern brushes, Scatter brushes don't distort the original image in any way.

Scatter brushes are far more versatile than they might at first seem. They can wildly scatter an object along a path, like confetti being thrown, or they can regimentally repeat an object along a path like ants on parade, and their sensitive settings mean you can do anything in between.

Making a new Scatter brush

New Scatter, Art, and Pattern brushes all have to start with a vector image. To keep things simple, we'll start with a triangle.

Next you need to make that shape become a brush. There are three ways to go about this:

1. **The drag and drop approach.** Simply select your shape and drag it into the Brushes palette.

2. **The menu option.** Select your object and then scroll down to New Brush in the palette menu.

3. **The New Brush icon.** Select your object and click on the New Brush icon at the bottom of the Brushes palette.

All three of these steps get you to the New Brush window. From here, check New Scatter Brush and click OK.

1.

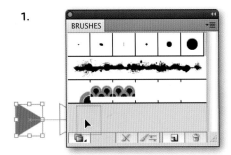

2.

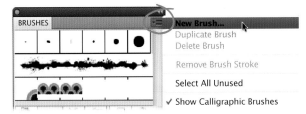

3.

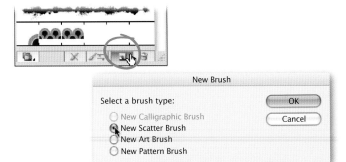

Scatter Brush Options

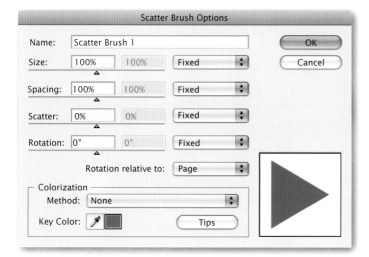

Size is the size of the objects compared with the original.

Spacing sets the space between each object on the path. Leave the slider on 100%, and each object will have a space which is roughly a sixth of the width of the original object between them. The higher the percentage the further apart each object will become, and the lower the percentage the closer together.

Scatter determines how far the object will go from the path the brush is applied to. A setting of 0% is on the path, but move the slider higher and the objects travel up on a horizontal path and to the right on a vertical path. Move the slider to a lower percentage, and the objects move down on a horizontal path and left on a vertical path.

The Scatter Brush Options window contains all the adjustments and settings for your brush. It will appear when you first create a Scatter brush, and can be accessed at any time by double-clicking on the brush in the Brushes palette.

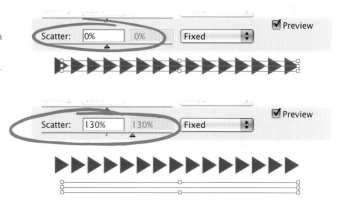

Rotation sets the angle of the objects compared with that of the original. Move the slider to the left and the object will rotate clockwise, move the slider to the right and the object will rotate counterclockwise.

Rotation relative to is not a slider setting, but a drop-down menu with two options: Rotation relative to Page and Rotation relative to Path. Choose Rotation relative to Page if you want all the objects on your path to point the same way (the same as the original object, when your Rotation slider is set to Fixed and positioned at 0°). Choose Rotation relative to Path if you want the objects to point in the direction of the path (when your slider is set to Fixed and positioned at 0°).

The last set of options in the Scatter Brush Options window are to do with Colorization. These are covered on pages 20 to 21.

The options menus

The options in the drop-down menus to the right of the sliders offer even more variation and take a little more explaining.

Fixed is the default setting, and means that all the objects on your path will be the same. Leaving your sliders on Fixed means you only get one point to drag to a percentage.

Random is, as it says, random, but you set the parameters. Choose Random from any of the menus and you get two points on the slider to play with. Slide these up and down to set the minimum and maximum variation levels. For example, if you select Random for the Size and then put one point at 50% and one at 200%, all the objects on a single path will be randomly sized between 50 and 200% of the size of your original object.

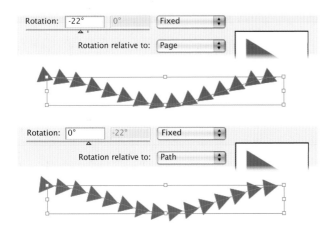

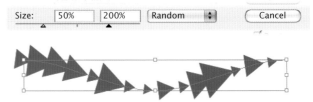

Sensitivity menu variants

The following five settings only work if you have a graphics pen and tablet and if you use them with the Paintbrush tool.

Pressure creates a brush where the objects vary depending on the pressure you apply when drawing the path with your pen.

The minimum value represents your lightest tablet pressure and the maximum value is the heaviest pressure. If you want there to be only a little variation, even when your pressure varies greatly, keep the two points close together. But if you want a large variation, and for the settings to be very sensitive to the pressure applied, then move the points on the slider further apart.

Out of the four graphics pen settings, Pressure is the easiest to use and is the most common feature available, as not all tablets can detect Tilt, Bearing, or Rotation.

Stylus Wheel can only be used if you have a pen with a stylus wheel. The stylus wheel on these pens controls the virtual ink flow, simulating an airbrush rather than a pen.

The Stylus Wheel setting means that the objects will vary depending on the position of the wheel on your pen as you draw.

Tilt varies the brush depending on the angle of your pen to the tablet.

Bearing varies the brush depending on where the tip of the brush is pointing.

Rotation varies the brush stroke depending on how the pen is rotated around the axes of the pen itself.

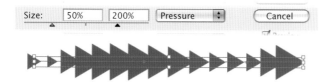

The two types of Scatter brush

At first it may seem that Scatter brushes are only good for one thing: scattering. However, they can create two quite different effects—the obvious scattered effect, and a much more uniform line. By changing the options, you can achieve these two effects with the same initial shape.

The first triangle brush has all its options set to Random and is definitely a scattered Scatter brush.

The second triangle brush has all its options set to fixed, which creates an orderly and repetitive brush.

Once you've mastered the basics, you can start to use the Scatter brush options to give your brushes appropriate characteristics. The Scattered effect is great for things that would naturally be scattered, such as confetti, a flock of birds, or clouds. It is also good for building up images in a haphazard way, like leaves on a tree.

The Orderly effect is one that people often overlook. If you want a simple shape to repeat but follow your path tightly, and not distort on a curved path, such as footsteps or stitches, then a Scatter brush is the perfect tool.

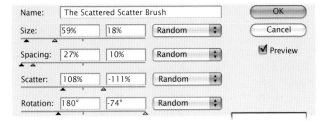

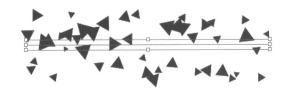

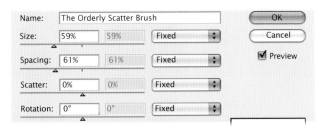

Scatter or Pattern?

Both Scatter and Pattern brushes can repeat a single object along a path. The difference between the two is that a Scatter brush won't distort or curve the original object to a curved path, and a Pattern brush will.

Which type of brush you choose depends on what type of effect you're after, and what the object is. Is it something that would bend, like an arrow, or something that would always remain in its original state, like a footprint?

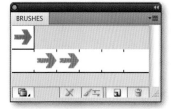

Scatter brush

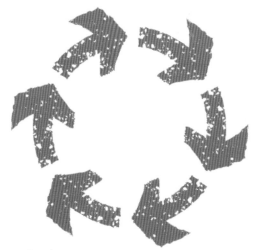

Pattern brush

Autumn Leaves 1

Try changing the Colorization method to Tints, and then overlaying this brush in different colors for a more dramatic fall scene.

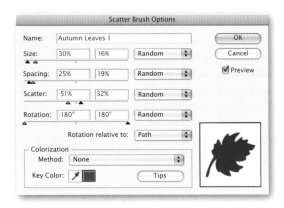

Autumn Leaves 2

These leaves look like they are blowing in the wind due to their random Size and Rotation settings.

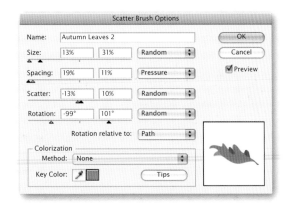

Falling Leaves 1

You can make these leaves fall further apart by increasing the distance between the two sliders on the Scatter bar.

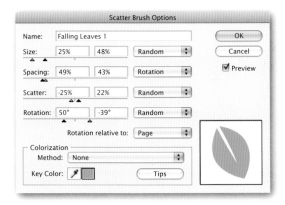

Falling Leaves 2

These leaves are a palmately compound leaf shape, found on maple, palm, and horse chestnut trees.

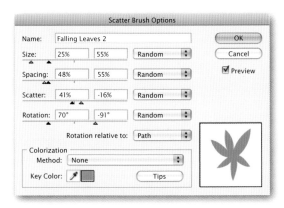

Dandelion 1

The seed head of this dandelion flower was created using
the Dandelion Seed 5 Scatter brush (see page 66).

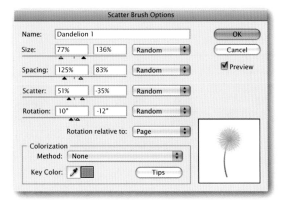

Dandelion 2

This realistic seed head was created by building up layers
of the Dandelion Seed 4 Scatter brush on circular paths
(see page 64).

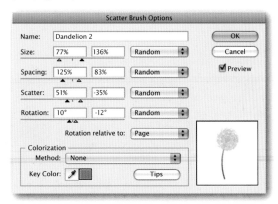

Dandelion Seed 1

These illustrated dandelion parachutes and seeds were created
using Live Trace in Illustrator.

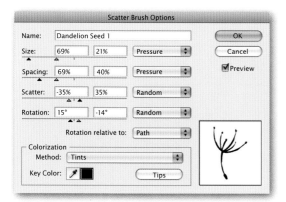

Dandelion Seed 2

With these delicate seed parachutes you can control the wind! Their Size and Spacing options are set to Pressure, which
means the harder you press with your graphics pen, the farther the parachutes scatter and the larger they become.

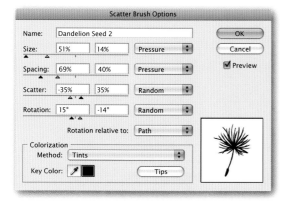

Dandelion Seed 3

Because of their shared style, you can combine Dandelion Seed 3 with
Dandelion Seed 4, for a more varied illustration.

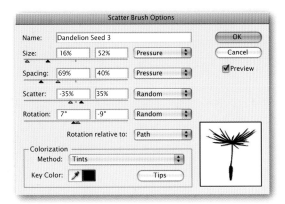

Dandelion Seed 4

Because there is no black in this brush and its Colorization method is set to
Hue Shift, these dandelion seeds will become the stroke color of your path.

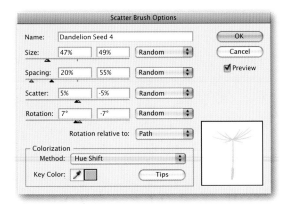

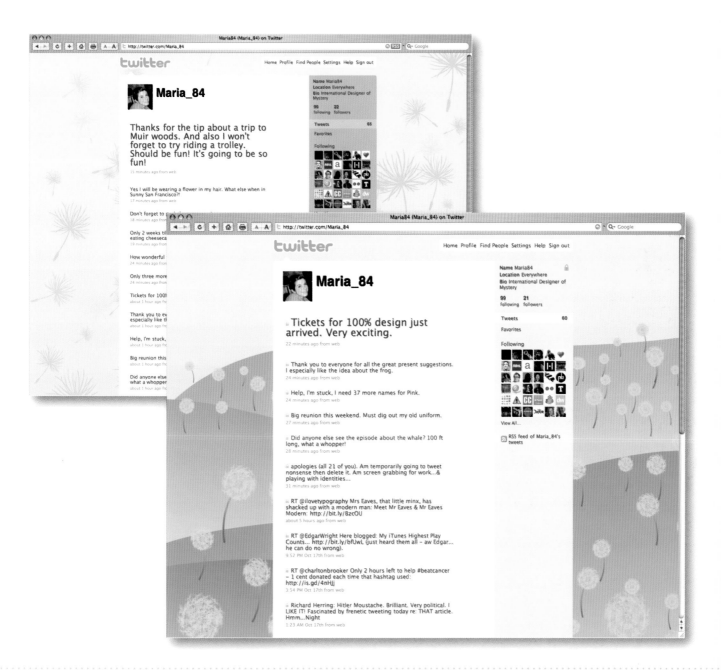

Background images for Twitter website created using Dandelion Seed 2 and Dandelion 2.

Dandelion Seed 5

This simple graphic seed can build up to make a very elaborate seed head by applying the brush to overlapping circular paths.

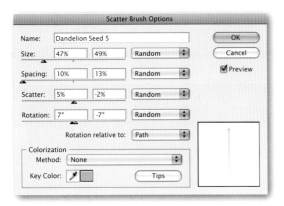

Blades of Grass 1

Because this bush has its Spacing set below 100%, the clumps of grass will slightly overlap on a path.

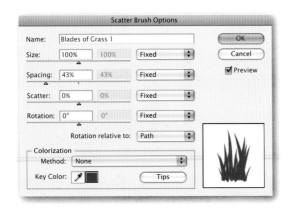

Blades of Grass 2

If you want to use this brush to create sporadic clumps of grass, increase the Spacing value to over 100%.

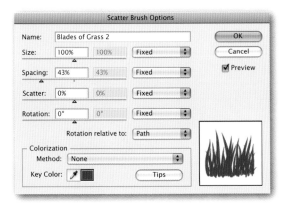

Flower Leaf

This semitransparent brush was created using an expanded gradient.

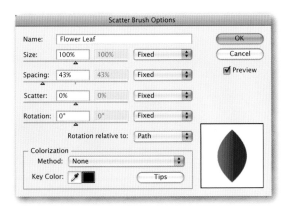

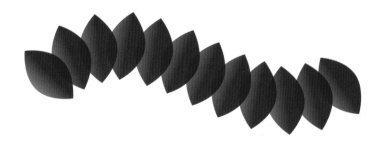

Petal

Even though this brush can change color (because its Colorization method is set to Tints), it will always maintain its gradient appearance.

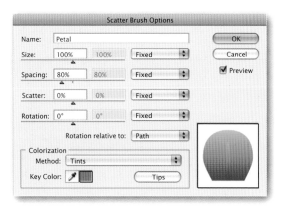

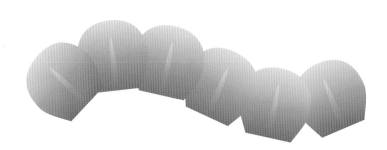

Rose Leaf

This brush works wonderfully when combined with the Rose Head 2 Scatter brush, as it is in the gift wrap featured on page 53.

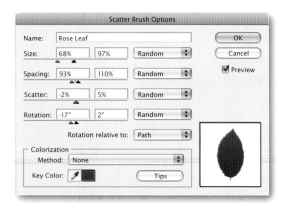

String of Beads

Since gradients can't be used in brushes, this brush was created using an Object Blend.

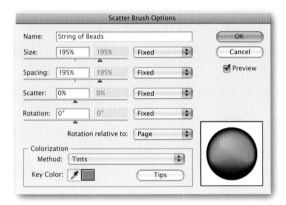

Pressure Pearls

If you have a graphics tablet, you can increase the size of these pearls by pressing down harder with your graphics pen.

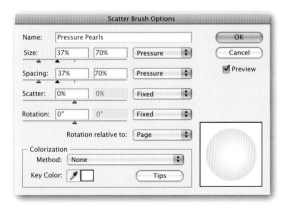

Hibiscus Flower Head

This brush's Colorization method is set to Tints and Shades, so you can change the color of the brush by changing the stroke color of the path it is applied to.

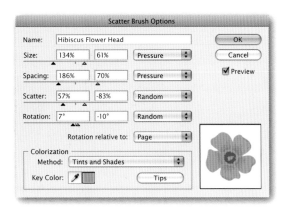

Cherry Blossom

Adapt the original artwork of this brush so that it is set to Multiply and about 80% Transparency, then save it as a new brush. When you draw over an image of skin, the brush takes on the appearance of a cherry blossom tattoo.

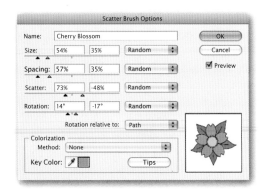

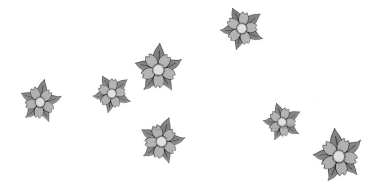

Rose Head 1

This brush has its Spacing option set to Pressure, so the harder you press with your graphics pen, the bigger the roses will become.

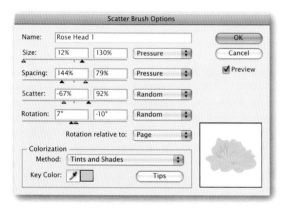

Rose Head 2

This pretty rose head has a vintage decoupage feel to it.

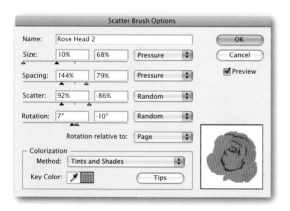

Bee 1

These bees fly in all directions because their Rotation option is set to Random, and the sliders are positioned at -24 and 99°.

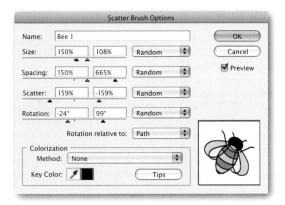

Bee 2

You can easily build a swarm of these bees by applying this brush to overlapping scribbled paths.

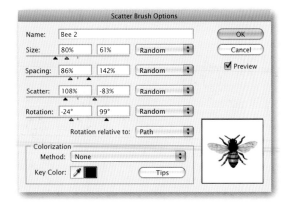

Ladybug 1

These are the common scarlet ladybugs (*Coccinellidae*) with small black spots on their wing covers.

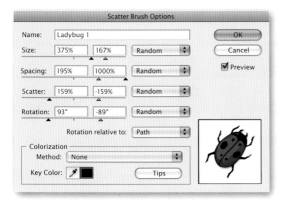

Ladybug 2

These flying ladybugs will always keep their original coloring, no matter what stroke color you choose, because their Colorization method is set to None.

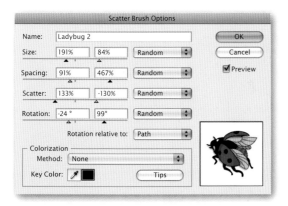

Beetles 1

These 1950s-illustration-style beetles look like they might be a bit lost, but change the Rotation setting from Random to Fixed and they will form an orderly procession.

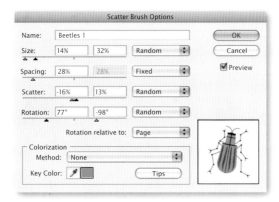

Butterfly 1

This brush has retained its hand-drawn feel because of the Live Trace setting used to turn the original drawing into a vector illustration.

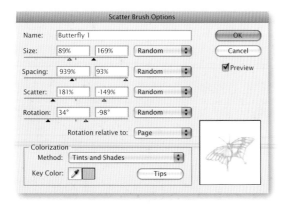

Butterfly 2

All of the Butterfly brushes are set to 95% Opacity and Multiply Blending Mode, so when they fly over each other their wings are semitransparent.

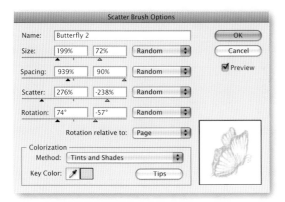

Butterfly 3

You can change the color of the Butterfly brushes, but they will always retain their pale shades because the original illustrations are in soft gray tones.

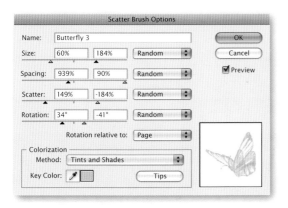

Fur

This brush creates an edge of fur, but if you want to create scatter clumps of fur, increase the Spacing value in the brush's Options window.

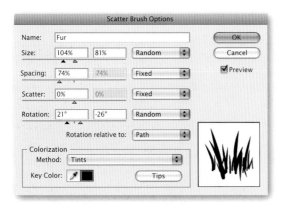

Bunnies

These rabbits randomly multiply, just like the real thing!

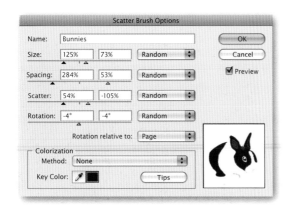

Brick

If you apply this brush to staggered straight paths, you can very quickly build a brick wall.

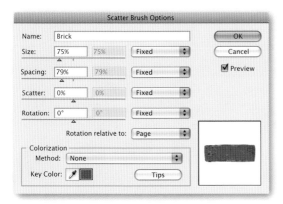

Lego Brick

These toy bricks will always keep their shading, no matter what color you make them.

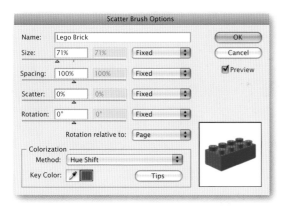

Sugar Candies 1

These bright candies were created with a Calligraphic brush and the Blob Brush tool.
A photo of candies was pasted onto its own Template layer in Illustrator, then painted over.

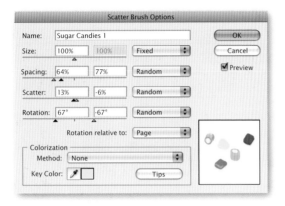

Sugar Candies 2

Once all the candies were drawn, they were divided into two clusters to make
two separate brushes, which could be overlaid for a more random scattering.

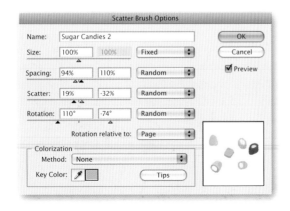

Day of the Dead Flowers

These bright and detailed flowers are inspired by the Day of the Dead celebrations in Mexico. They can be built up to form a beautiful floral tribute.

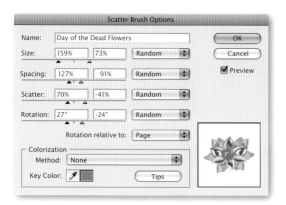

Chocolate Candies

These candies keep their brightness whatever stroke color you apply to them because the original is bright red and the Colorization method is set to Hue Shift.

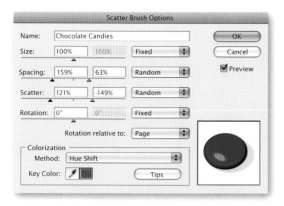

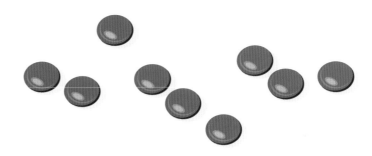

Paisley 1

This is a dainty paisley border, but you can easily recolor it with stronger
tones for a more striking look or with natural browns for a henna effect.

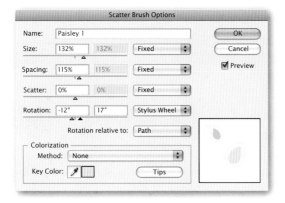

Falling Feather

The illustration which made this brush was set to Multiply and 58% Transparency and was colored
using an expanded gradient—all of which helps to give it a realistic and airy look.

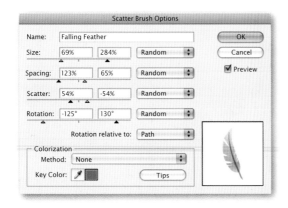

Slanted Arrows

These comic-book-style arrows are useful elements for logos,
paths on maps, flow charts, or comic strips.

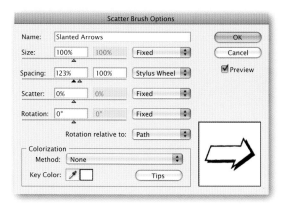

Printed Arrows

These arrows might have a rough, printed look, but their brush options are uniformly set to Fixed
to create a brush similar to a Pattern brush, but with no distortion of the original illustration.

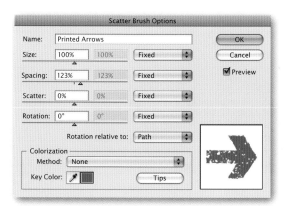

Random Arrows

The Spacing and Scatter options for this brush are both set to Pressure, so the harder you press down with your graphics pen, the further apart the arrows become from each other, and the path they are on.

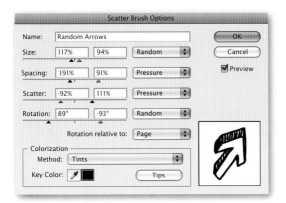

Stack of Coins

These coins stack with no space between them because their Spacing option has been set to 12%; at 100% there would still be space between them when they are placed on a vertical path.

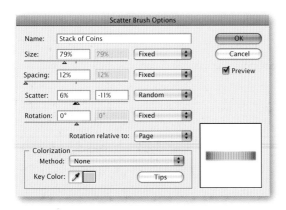

Live Trace Coin

The original coin illustration which was used to make this brush was created from a photograph, which was then vectorized using the Live Trace function in Illustrator.

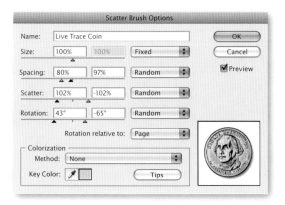

Dream Plus

The Random settings of this brush mean you get a great variety of Size and Spacing, which gives the feeling of depth and perspective.

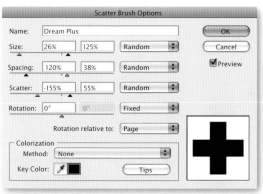

Design: Ilias Sounas

Dream Circles 1

The close range of both the Spacing and Scatter options for this brush mean these graphic circles overlap in a random manner.

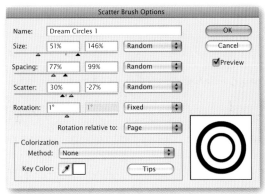

Design: Ilias Sounas

Dream Circles 2

Both Dream Circles brushes are used in the creation of the Follow Your Dreams illustration on page 52.

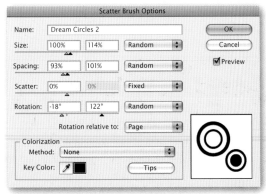

Design: Ilias Sounas

Heart Plus

These randomly scattered crosses will always appear at the same angle, no matter what shape path they are applied to, because their Rotation method is set to Fixed relative to Page.

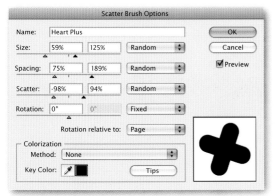

Design: Ilias Sounas

Heart Raindrops

These raindrops are currently black, but if you want them to take on a more blueish tone, you can either change their Colorization method or adapt the original artwork.

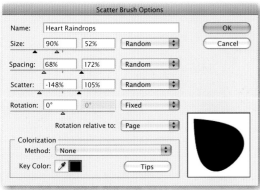

Design: Ilias Sounas

Powerball Fragments

This jagged brush was used in the creation of the Powerball illustration on page 252.

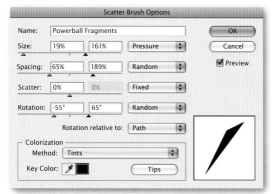

Scatter Brush Options

Name: Powerball Fragments

Size: 19% 161% Pressure

Spacing: 65% 189% Random

Scatter: 0% 0% Fixed

Rotation: -55° 65° Random

Rotation relative to: Path

Colorization
Method: Tints
Key Color: Tips

OK
Cancel
☑ Preview

Design: André SMATIK Ljosaj

Cumulus

These fluffy clouds can change shade with the stroke color, but they will always be light because of the light colors in the original brush artwork.

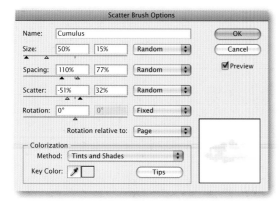

Scatter Brush Options

Name: Cumulus

Size: 50% 15% Random

Spacing: 110% 77% Random

Scatter: -51% 32% Random

Rotation: 0° 0° Fixed

Rotation relative to: Page

Colorization
Method: Tints and Shades
Key Color: Tips

OK
Cancel
☑ Preview

Stratus

These long, streaky clouds tend to hang around below 6,000 feet (1,828m).

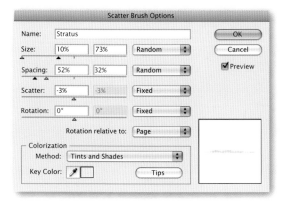

Altocumulus

The appearance of these clouds on a warm, humid summer morning often means thunderstorms may occur by late afternoon.

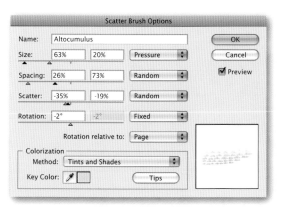

Marbles 1

These semitransparent marbles will take on any stroke color and keep their transparency because the original illustration was grayscale, and their Colorization method is set to Tints.

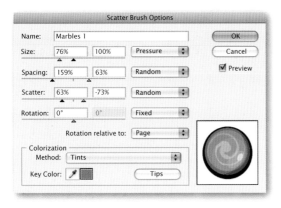

Marbles 2

These marbles can be transformed into bubbles by lowering the transparency of the original illustration and recreating the brush.

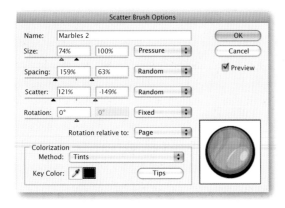

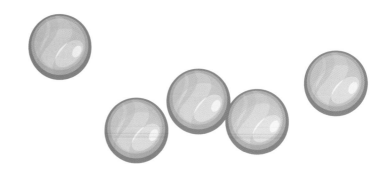

Stitches

A dashed line will create a simple stitches effect, but this brush has a
thread design which makes it more realistic, even on close inspection.

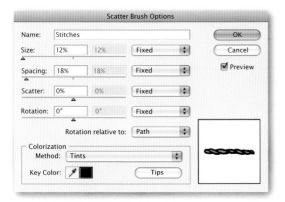

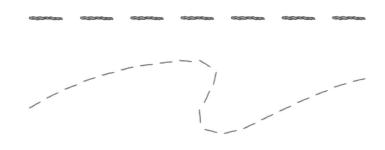

Cross-Stitch

Because the original illustration is grayscale and the Colorization is set to Tints,
the stroke detail of this brush will always be a stronger tone of the inside fill color.

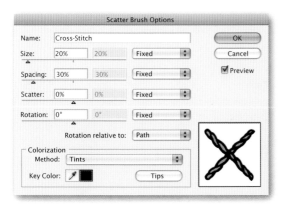

Tattoo Sparrows

Although the original drawing is in a traditional tattoo blue, you can change the color of these little birds to anything you like because the Colorization method is set to Hue Shift.

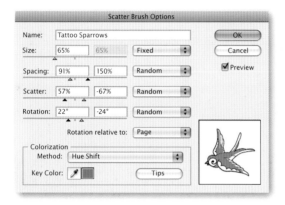

Starling in Flight 1

These silhouetted birds look great overlaid on a photo of the sky, as they are in the illustration on page 52.

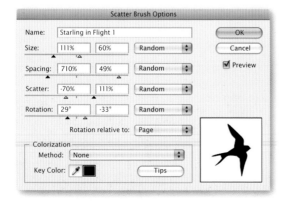

Starling in Flight 2

If you want to change the color of these birds, you'll need to change
the original drawing from black, or change their Colorization method.

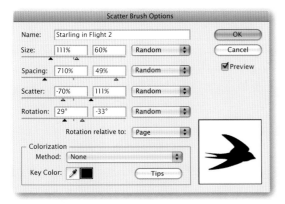

Starling in Flight 3

Combine all the Starling in Flight brushes to create a flock
swarming in the sky.

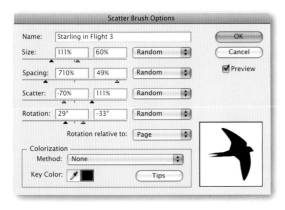

Triangle Confetti

This simple yet effective brush has its Colorization method set to Tints, so you can vary the color of overlaid strokes for realistic-looking confetti.

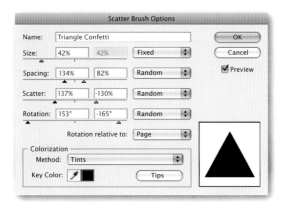

Heart Confetti

Although both Spacing and Scatter are set to Random for these brushes, the sliders are carefully positioned to give a realistic, scattered look.

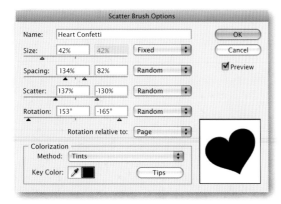

Horse Shoe Confetti

Mix the Triangle, Heart, and Horse Shoe Confetti brushes together with different stroke colors for truly random confetti.

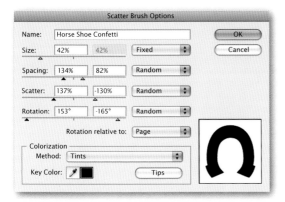

Mixed Confetti

If you want a scattering that comes premade, try this cluster of different-colored confetti.

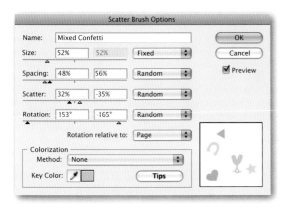

Button 1

Both Button brushes will always be lighter shades of your chosen stroke color because the original brush artwork is shades of gray, rather than black.

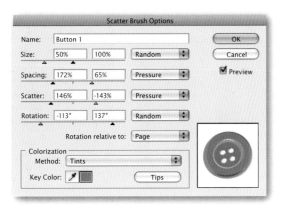

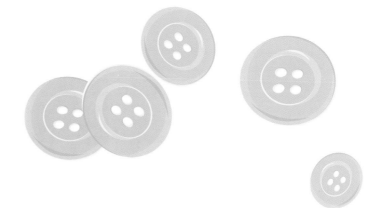

Button 2

These Button brushes scatter further from your path the harder you press with your graphics pen. If you don't have a graphics pen, the buttons will always scatter to the maximum value your Spacing and Scatter sliders are set to.

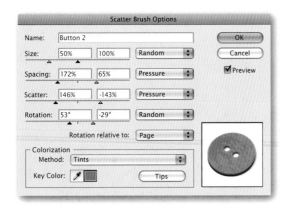

Cup Cakes

These cute cup cakes sit at random, jaunty angles, creating a pretty border or irregular pattern depending on the type of path you apply them to.

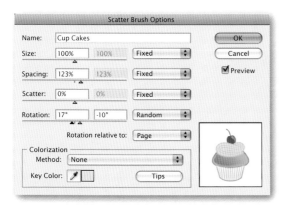

Muffins

These muffins were created using an Object Blend and the cases are shaded with a mix of Highlight and Contour Line Art brushes.

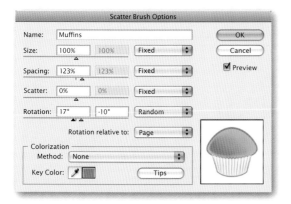

Piped Frosting

Perfect for decorating cakes and muffins.

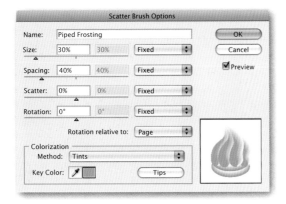

Coffee Ring 1

These coffee-cup marks look realistic because they were live traced from photographs.

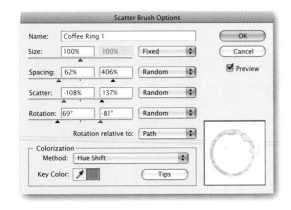

Coffee Ring 2

This brush makes it look like you have put your cup down wherever you please, because the Spacing and Scatter options are both set to Random.

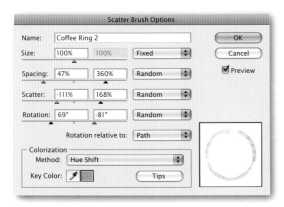

Coffee Ring 3

Change the stroke color of your path to a deep shade of red to create wine glass rings instead of coffee.

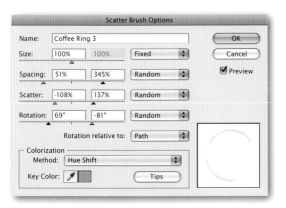

Rivets

A good example of a nonscattered Scatter brush.

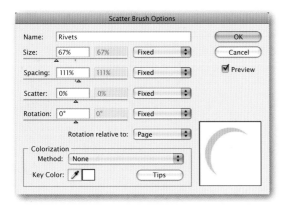

Sequins

These sequins look great scattered against a dark background. Build them up and you can completely cover any garment for maximum glitz effect.

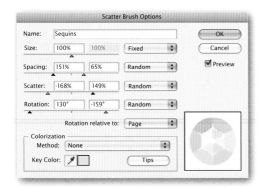

Fluffy Cloud

The original cloud illustration used to make this brush was created using
an expanded gradient and set to 80% Opacity for a fluffy, ethereal look.

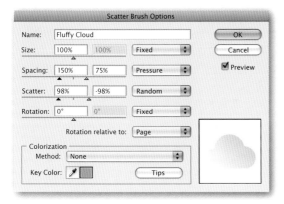

Rainy Cloud

The Spacing for this brush is set to Pressure, so the harder you press, the further apart the rainy
clouds become. If you don't have a graphics pen and tablet, change the Spacing to Random.

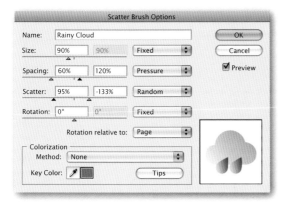

Mixing colors tutorial

For some Scatter brushes, like candies or marbles, you may want a selection of colors all mixed together.

There are two ways to do this. You can make a cluster of objects each in a different color, and then load the cluster into a Scatter brush. The problem with this is the different colors will always be in the same position, so what should look random starts to look like a pattern. However, this is the best option if you also want a mix of shapes as well as colors, as in the Mixed Confetti brush (see page 93).

If you don't want a mix of shapes, the alternative is to set your brush Colorization method to Tints.

Marbles come in a rainbow of colors, and they are also semitransparent, so ideally you want to be able to create a mix of colors which can be seen through each other, when they overlap.

1.   Draw your marble and color it using black, white, and shades of gray. Use black for the area you eventually want to have the strongest color, and use white on the areas you want to stay white.

2.   Select all the elements in your marble and group them together: Object > Group (⌘ + G) so that you can change the transparency of the marble as a whole.

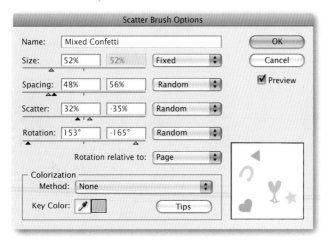

3. Adjust the Transparency setting to 90% Opacity.

4. Now create a new Scatter brush from your marble illustration.

5. Change the Colorization mode to Tints. When set to Tints, any parts of your marble that are black will become the stroke color, any parts that are gray will become tints of the stroke color, and the white parts will remain white.

6. When you're happy with your brush options, name your brush and click OK.

7. With your new brush selected, draw a number of different strokes that overlap each other. Then change the stroke color for each path. You will get a scattering of colored marbles, all with a glassy effect.

Tip:
It is usually a good idea to group all the elements within an illustration before making it any type of brush, just to make sure no elements get nudged out of place.

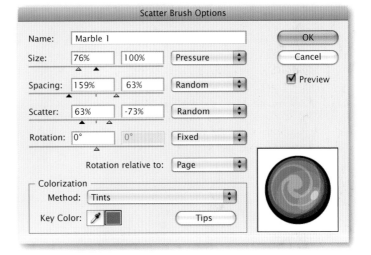

Art brushes

1

KERSVERS PRESENTS

FRIZZ
CONTROL

BY VIA GRAFIK

MUSIC BY DJ CLYDE

AT TOMMY'Z TOKO
ADMIRAAL DE RUIJTERWEG 85
AMSTERDAM

OPENING 19 DECEMBER 2008
18:00 - 22:00

3

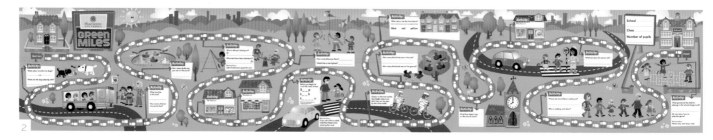

2

4

5

6

1. **Brush Type Collection by Adam Lewis**
Adam Lewis' experimental collection of display typefaces was created by adding brush strokes to fonts until the original fonts were no longer recognizable.

2. **Green Miles poster by David Caunce**
Art brushes were used for the path and footprint of this poster designed to encourage school children to travel to school by means other than a car.

3. **Frizz Control flyer by André Nossek and Leo Volland**
The hair ball background of this flyer was created with Art brushes designed specifically for this project.

4. **Alley by Julian James**
Julian created this illustration with a mix of original Art and Pattern brushes to feature in a self-promotional piece.

5. **Bottles illustration by Emily Portnoi**
Simple flat bottles have been lifted with a mixture of the Highlight and Half Highlight Art brushes.

6. **Culture Online logo by David Caunce**
Designed for the UK's Department of Culture, Media and Sport, this logo was created with a specially-designed Art brush made up of a series of squares.

Art brushes explained

Where Calligraphic brushes end, Art brushes start. Calligraphic brushes can replicate beautiful calligraphy nibs, but with Art brushes you can make your stroke look like it was created by just about anything.

An Art brush places a single object/illustration along a path. It is possible to have that shape keep its original proportions or you can choose to have it stretch to fit your path. It is important to bear this in mind when designing an Art brush, since your original object may become distorted—will it still work?

Making a new Art brush

Art brushes are made in exactly the same way as Scatter brushes. You have to start by creating the vector illustration that will become your brush. Once you're happy with your illustration, there are three ways to turn your illustration into an Art brush:

1. **The drag and drop approach.** Simply select your shape and drag it into the Brushes palette.

2. **The menu option.** Select your object and then scroll down to New Brush in the palette menu.

3. **The New Brush icon.** Select your object and click on the New Brush icon at the bottom of the Brushes palette.

All three of these steps get you to the New Brush window. From here, check New Art Brush and click OK.

1.

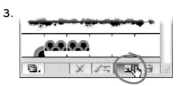

2.

3.

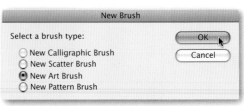

Art Brush Options

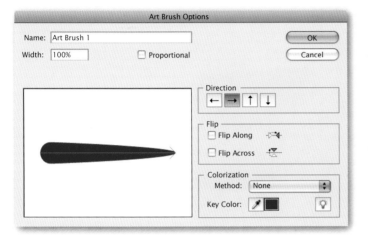

The Art Brush Options window allows you to control the scale, proportion, color mode, and direction of your Art brush.

Width adjusts the width of your brush compared with your original object. 100% is as per your original object, but you can adjust this to be anything from 1% to 10,000%. It won't affect the length, because that is determined by your path.

Proportional means that, when checked, both the length and width of your brush strokes will always be scaled up or down in proportion to your original object. When unchecked a brush will stretch lengthways to fit a longer path, and compress to fit a shorter path, but the width will remain the same.

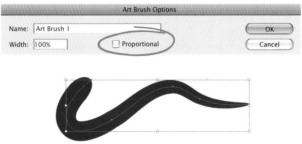

Direction determines in which direction your original object will be placed along your path in relation to the direction you draw in. There are four Direction options: stroke from right to left (arrow left), stroke from left to right (arrow right), stroke from bottom to top (arrow upwards), and stroke from top to bottom (arrow downwards).

The easiest way to think about it is, which part of the brush do you want to be placed at the beginning of your path— the right side, left side, top, or bottom? For example, if the direction is set to right, it means that the left-hand edge of your brush will always be placed at the beginning of your path. If you draw a path from left to right, the brush will be placed from left to right, but if you draw a path from right to left, the brush will be placed right to left, because it always starts with the left-hand edge of the brush.

The default direction of your brush is determined by your original object. If your original object is landscape, then the direction will be to the right, if it's portrait, then it will automatically be downward.

The brush preview in the Options window has a thin, blue arrow over the top of your brush, showing the direction selected.

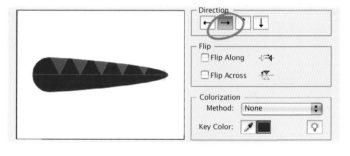

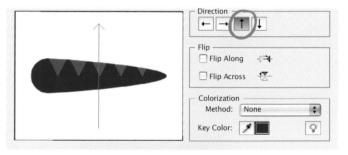

Flip: these two options can change the direction of your brush on a path.

- **Flip Along** vertically changes the orientation of your brush in relation to your path. When you have your direction set to either right or left, checking Flip Along is essentially the same as changing between horizontal direction modes. However, if you have your direction set to up or down, then checking Flip Along reflects your brush artwork vertically, while maintaining the direction set.

- **Flip Across** horizontally changes the orientation of your brush in relation to your path. When you have your direction set to either up or down, checking Flip Across is essentially the same as changing between vertical direction modes. However, if you have your direction set to left or right, then checking Flip Across reflects your brush artwork horizontally, while maintaining the direction set.

  Neither Flip mode is reflected in the brush preview.

Colorization is covered on pages 20 to 21.

Preview will show you how your settings will affect your brush on any existing path it is applied to.

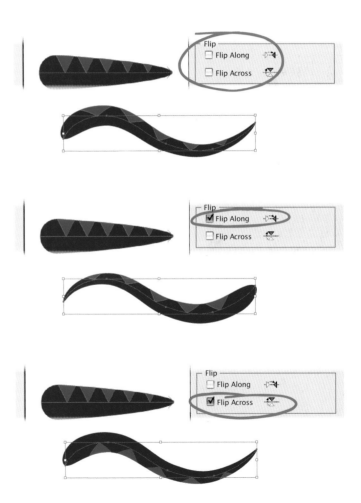

Flying Blocks 1

These cartoon-style blocks can be made to fly about all over the place. Mix them with Flying Blocks 2 for a more random effect.

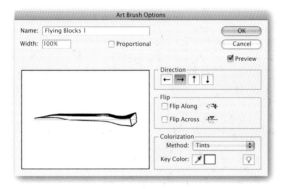

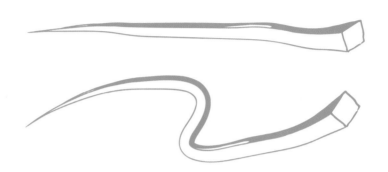

Flying Blocks 2

These swirly blocks get their cartoon look from being originally drawn in an inky-style Art brush.

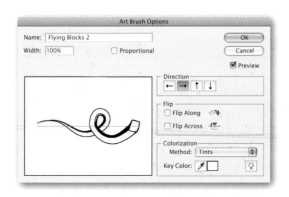

Swirls 1

This pretty ornamental brush was created using a tapered Art brush.

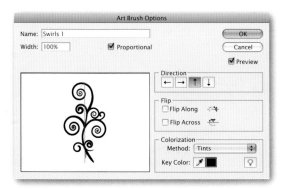

Swirls 2

These Swirls brushes will change to the stroke color in your color palette, because the original brush artwork is black and the Colorization method is set to Tints.

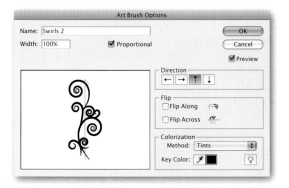

Heart 1

A simple Art brush that started life as a drawing and was then scanned in and transformed into a vector illustration through the Live Trace feature in Illustrator.

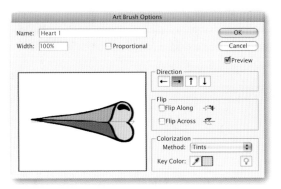

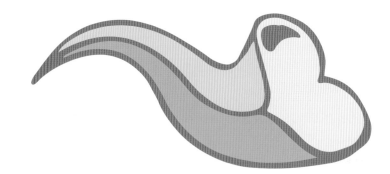

Heart 2

This brush will always keep the same contrasting tones, which give it its 3D look, because the original brush is colored with shades of gray and the Colorization method is set to Tints.

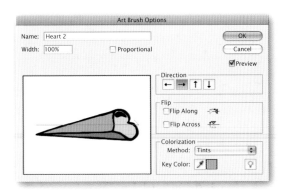

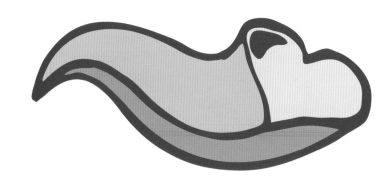

Hand Lines 1 & 2

Hand Lines 1 & 2 are the same shape, but 1 is filled with a tint, and 2 is only outlines.

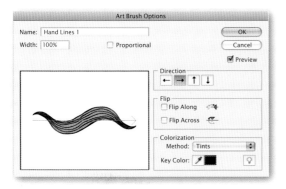

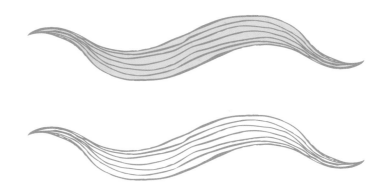

Hand Lines 3

This third brush in the Hand Lines series is open-ended and is only made up of outlines.

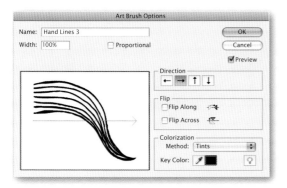

Locks 1 & 2

Both Locks brushes are exactly the same shape and both have their Colorization method set to Tints, but 1 has a gray fill and 2 is only outlines.

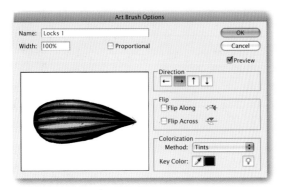

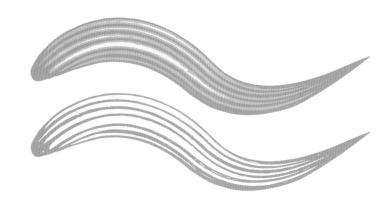

Cactus

This spiky cactus arm can be built up to create a monster cactus plant.

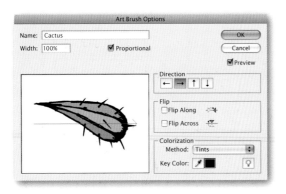

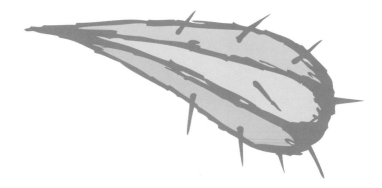

Strand 1

This twisted lock can be used as hair, tentacles, leaves, and more.

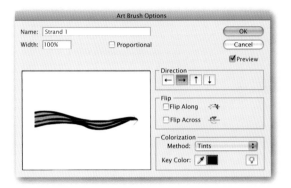

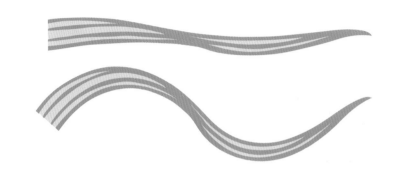

Strand 2

Because of its direction setting, this brush will always start with the wide, flat base and end with the tip of the strand—no matter which direction you draw in.

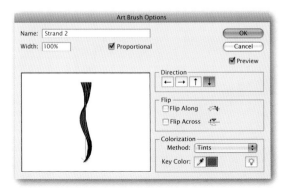

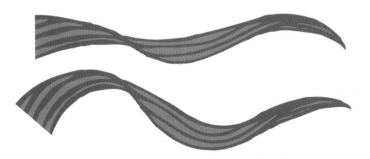

Strand 3

Layering strokes of this brush can build up a healthy head of hair.

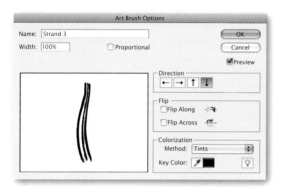

Strand 4

Because the original artwork is black, white, and gray, and its Colorization method
is set to Tints, this brush will always take on various shades of the stroke color.

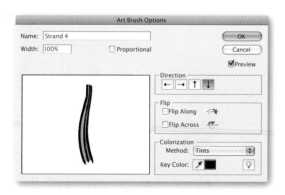

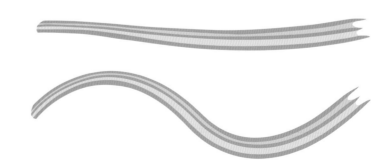

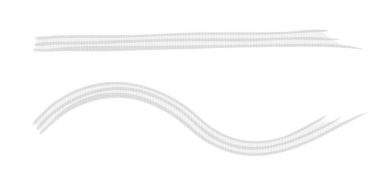

Strand 5

Combining the various Strands brushes can achieve a more realistic-looking hair illustration.

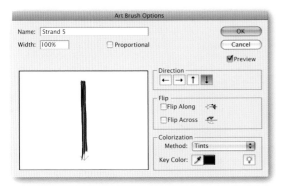

Strand 6

All the Strand brushes started life as hand-drawn illustrations, which is why they have natural irregularities in their shapes.

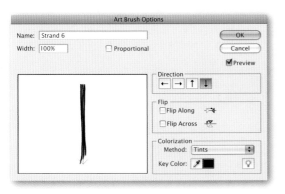

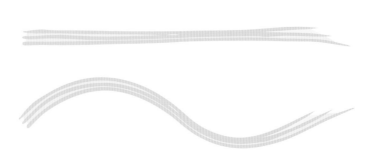

Woodblock

This brush has lots of printed detail, so any images made using it will have large file sizes. But it's well worth it for the realistic effect it produces.

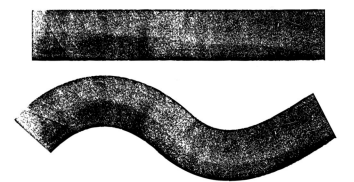

Pencil

A textured pencil line, which, when used thin, can give a sketched look to any vector illustration.

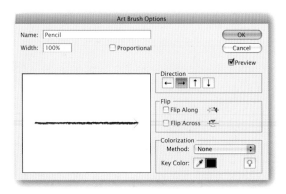

Pen

Because this pen is a brush rather than just a vector illustration, you can
animate it in any way you choose by applying it to different-shaped paths.

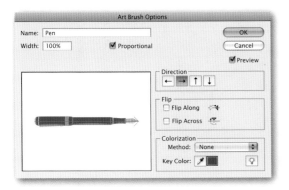

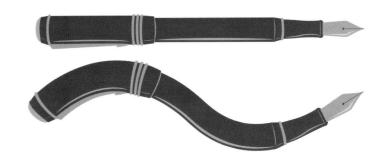

Splatter Paintbrush 1

The length and detail of this brush give the path a more realistic look.

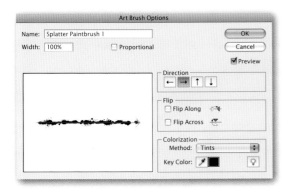

Branch

The inside of the leaves on this brush will never take a color, but they will always stay opaque, so you can overlay branches without creating a mess of lines.

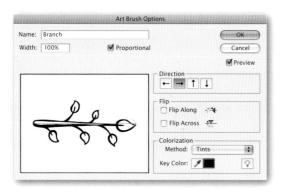

Thorny Branch

This brush is set to Proportional, so the longer your path, the wider the brush will become.

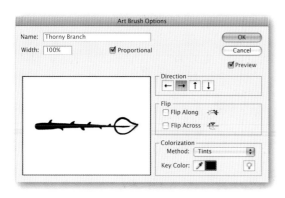

Twisted Branch

Art brushes don't like to be twisted or looped on a single path, they sometimes cancel themselves out, so this brush comes with the twists already in.

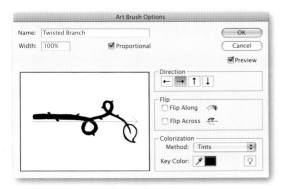

Rose 1 & 2

This brush has two versions: 1 is outline only and 2 is filled. Both are set to Proportional, so the taller the rose stem, the bigger the flower.

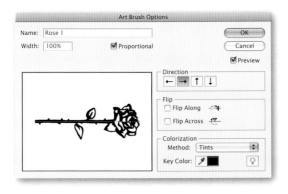

Two Leaf Stem

This elegant stem can create beautiful foliage.

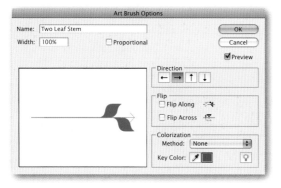

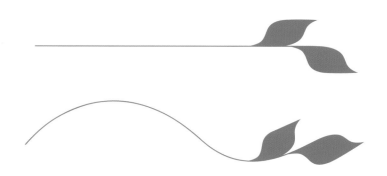

Curled Stem

This pretty brush comes in bright red, but if you want to change its color, you either have to change its Colorization method or adapt the original artwork.

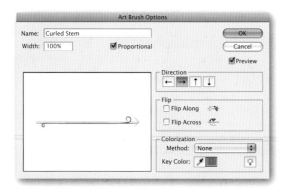

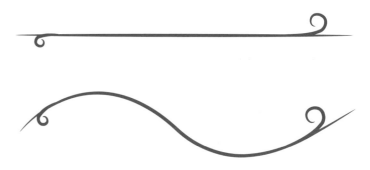

Stalk

This brush is great for finishing off illustrations of fruit or flowers.

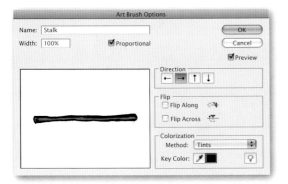

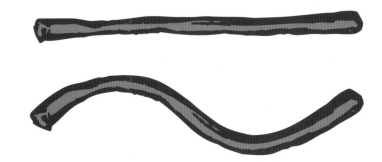

Swirly Leaf

This growing vine started life as a pencil drawing, which was converted to a vector illustration using Live Trace.

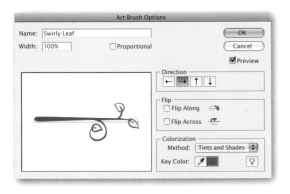

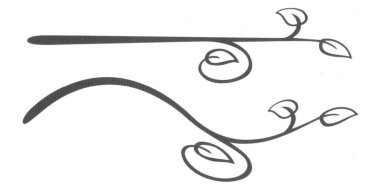

Chinese Brush 1

This irregular stroke is perfect for creating Chinese-style lettering.

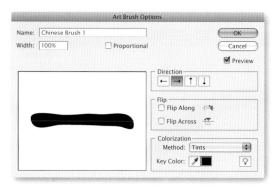

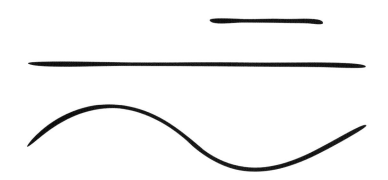

Chinese Brush 2

All four Chinese Brushes are set to Tints, so you can decide what color ink to use, but black and red are traditional.

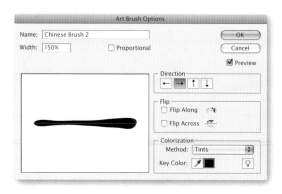

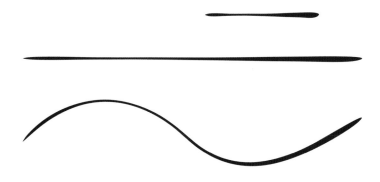

Chinese Brush 3

The four Chinese Brushes work best when combined with each other, giving more authentic differences between the brush strokes.

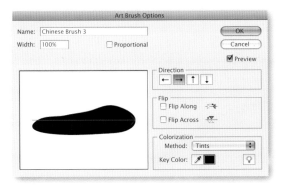

Chinese Brush 4

Change your stroke weight of a path to individually adjust the width of the brush applied to it, or alter the Width in the Option of Selected Object window.

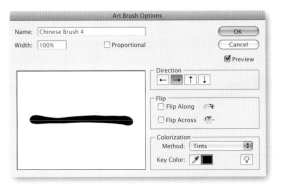

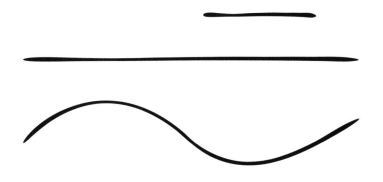

Chinese Watercolor Brush 1

These Chinese Watercolor Brushes were all created using an Object Blend.

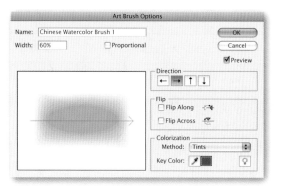

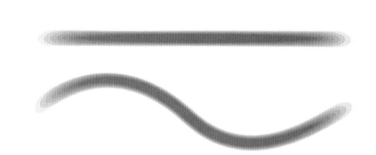

Chinese Watercolor Brush 2

The original illustrations for these Chinese Watercolor Brushes are all set to 75% Opacity and Blending Mode Darken, which helps give them their watery effect.

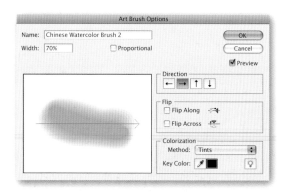

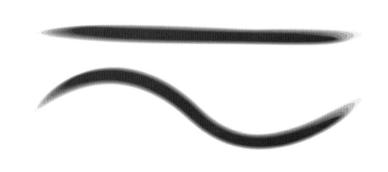

亮善和睦

Illustration by Emily Portnoi. Chinese Brush 1, 2, 3, and 4 were used to create the lettering and illustration for this image, while Chinese Watercolor Brush 1 and 2 created the shading.

Chinese Watercolor Brush 3

These brushes can become any watery shade you want because
their Colorization method is set to Tints.

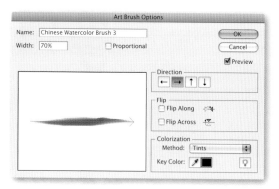

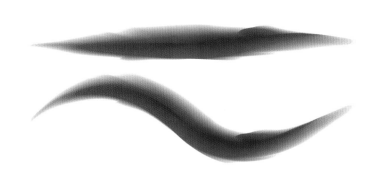

Chinese Watercolor Brush 4

You can make this brush wider or narrower by adjusting its Width option,
but its length will always be dictated by the path it's applied to .

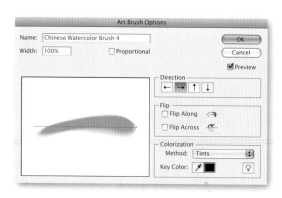

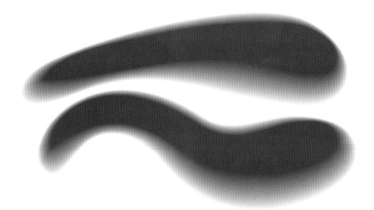

Soft Frosting

This brush was made using an Object Blend, and is great for decorating cakes. What's more, whatever color frosting you choose, it will always be a pastel shade, because the original brush artwork is made from shades of soft gray.

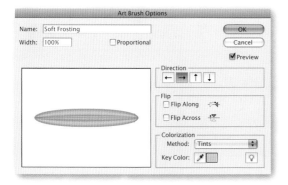

Airplane Trail

These two tapering strokes make great trails in the sky. This is a great brush for overlaying on photographs.

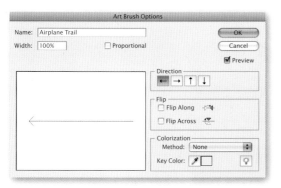

Growing Street Lamp

This urban street lamp can shrink to a vanishing point on a street, by making the paths you apply it to smaller and smaller.

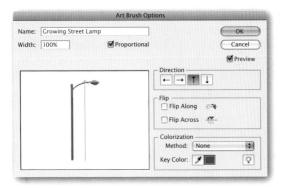

Silver D-Shaped Wire

This brush replicates the type of silver used to make jewelry, and was used in the creation of the clasp in the Pearls with Clasp brushes featured on page 215.

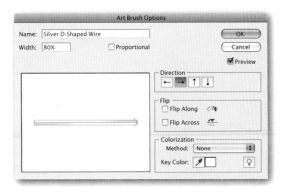

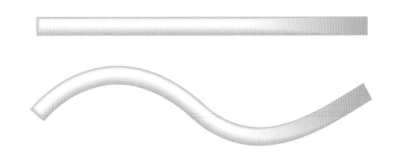

Perspective High-Rise

Because these brushes are set to Proportional, the shorter your path the smaller the building, and the further away it will seem.

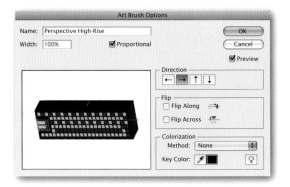

Perspective Apartment Building

If you turn off Proportional for these brushes, the buildings will become stretched.

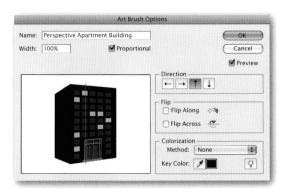

Contour Line

This brush is great for adding shading and shape to your illustrations.

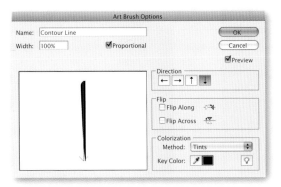

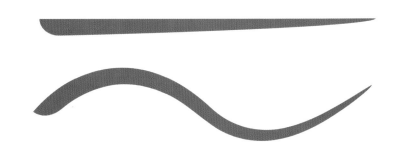

Highlighted Stroke

This brush can be great for lettering and creating borders, or if you just want a stroke that feels a little more 3D. Its Colorization method is set to Tints so the stroke can be any color you choose, but the highlights will always stay white.

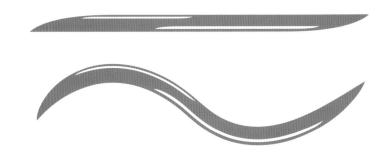

Highlight

This brush was used to give a shine to the Bottle illustration on page 103.

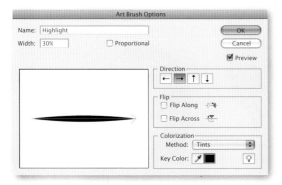

Half Highlight

This brush can be the quickest way to add highlights to hair.

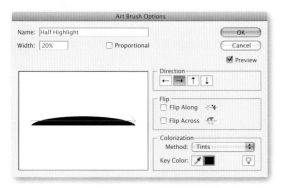

Growing Paisley

The longer your stroke, the bigger this paisley pattern will become.
To ensure that the shape doesn't distort, it's best applied to straight paths.

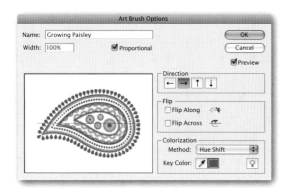

Wind

Apply these fluffy clouds to a straight path and you have a calm day,
but apply them to a waved path, and the wind instantly picks up.

Design: Ben the Illustrator

Growing Mountain

This Art brush makes great use of the Proportional setting.

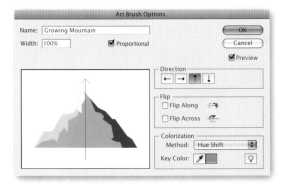

Elephant Family

These elephants on procession were made using an Object Blend.

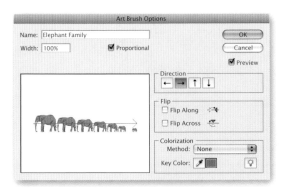

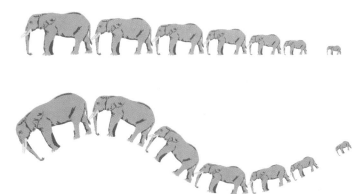

Yellow & Red Mushrooms

These two fungi brushes are both exactly the same, but with different color caps.

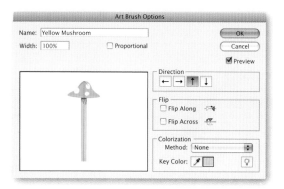

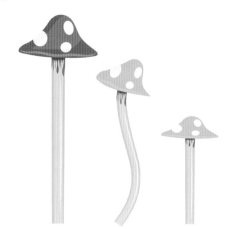

Shadow Mushroom

This brush has a semitransparent shadow. To see how it was created, refer to the Drop Shadow tutorial on page 236.

Growing Blade of Grass 1

Because this brush is set to grow proportionally, the longer the path you apply it to, the larger your blade of grass will become.

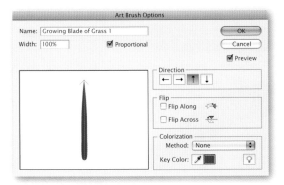

Growing Blade of Grass 2

This wild, twisted grass also works as seaweed, water reeds, or plant leaves.

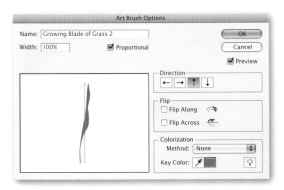

Leaf Taper

This leaf-shaped brush works wonderfully on short strokes
or stretched on a long spiral.

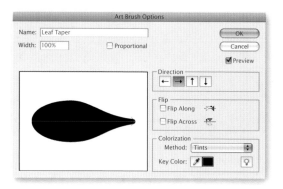

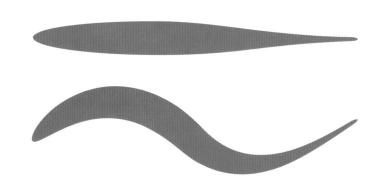

Ornamental Swirl

This woodblock-style ornament was created by Live Tracing a pencil sketch.

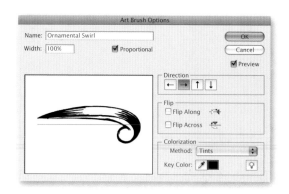

Ornamental Leaf 1

This half leaf works beautifully when added to a swirly path.

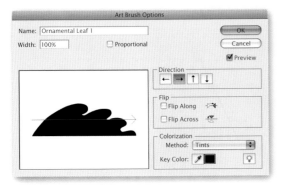

Ornamental Leaf 2

These ornamental leaves will stretch in length but not width, because they are not set to grow proportionally.

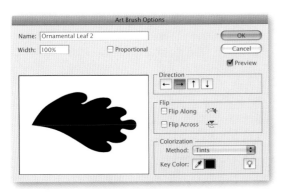

Ornamental Leaf 3

All three Ornamental Leaf brushes have their direction set toward the right, so the base of the leaves will always be at the start of your path, and the tip of the leaves at the end.

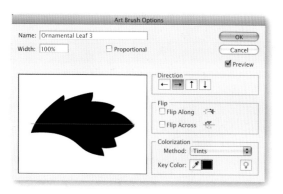

Rococo Leaf

This decorative leaf is inspired by the 18th-century French art and interior design style, rococo.

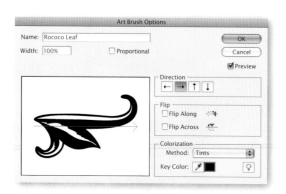

Rococo Leaf Detail 1

Natural patterns such as leaves were used to great effect in the rococo style.

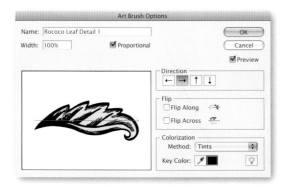

Rococo Leaf Detail 2

Both Rococo Leaf Detail brushes will change color with your stroke color. What is black in the original brush artwork will become the stroke color, and what is gray will be a tint of the stroke color.

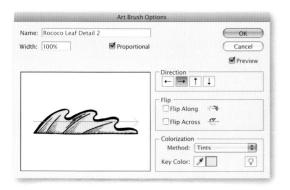

Rococo Leaves and Stem

This brush is a simplified version of the type of decorative leaves found in the interior and furniture design of the rococo period.

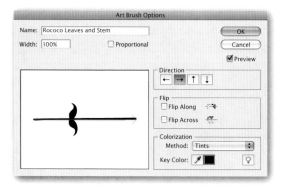

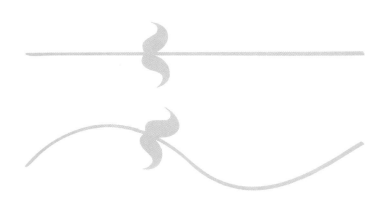

Rococo Leaf and Stem

This rococo-style leaf detail has a natural woodblock feel to it because it started life as a hand-drawn sketch.

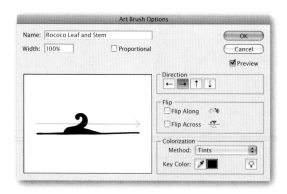

Arabesque Leaf 1

These beautifully detailed leaves add great drama to a design.

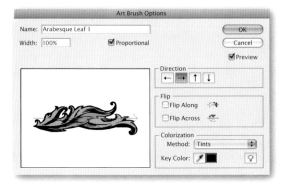

Arabesque Leaf 2

Because of the amount of detail in this brush, you have to be careful with it on long paths, as it will distort.

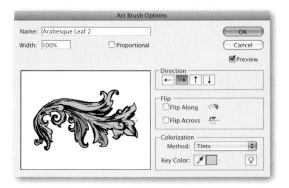

Daub 1

These simple Daub brushes are very flexible graphic elements, which can be combined together to great effect.

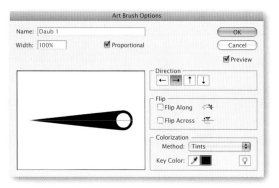

Daub 2

All the Daub brushes are set to Proportional, so will grow bigger on longer paths.

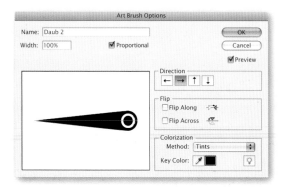

Daub 3

Each Daub brush has its direction set toward the right, so the point of the daubs will always
sit at the beginning of your path no matter which direction you draw in.

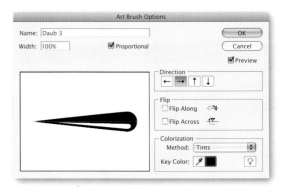

Daub 4

Because the original artwork for the Daub brushes only contains black and white, and their Colorization method
is set to Tints, the black will always be a 100% tint of whatever the stroke color is and the white will stay white.

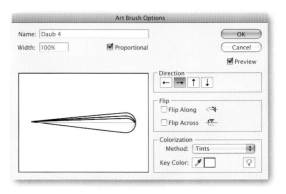

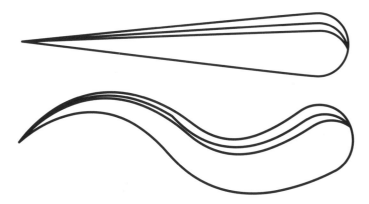

Daub 5

If you overlap this brush on different paths, you will not be able to see through the strokes because the brush has a solid white fill.

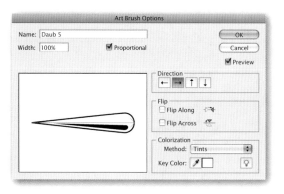

Petrol Daub

This highly-colored brush has some transparent elements in it, so when overlaid it retains its petrol-like quality.

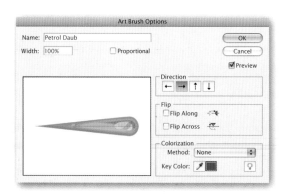

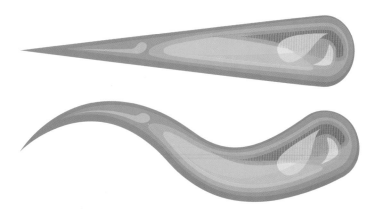

Architectural Wedge

This brush was used in the creation of the Growing Ionic Column Pattern brush on page 219.

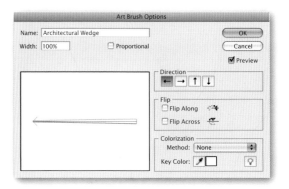

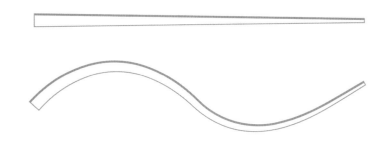

Wobbled Wedge

A simple brush, which is wide at one end and narrow at the other, with the look of a brush stroke or felt pen.

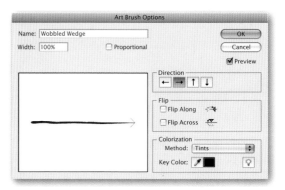

Wedge

A simple brush, but it can achieve great graphic effects—how else can you make absolutely any path wider at one end and narrower at the other?

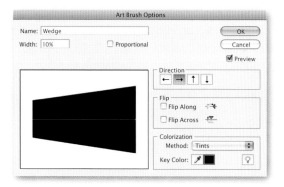

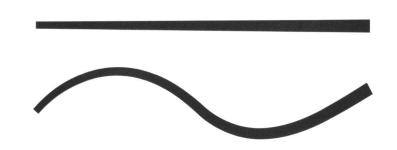

Asymmetric Wedge

The current direction of this brush is to the right, meaning that, no matter which direction you draw your path in, the start will always be thin and the end will always be thick.

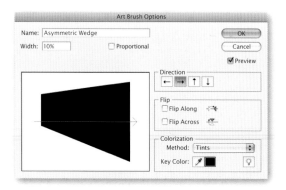

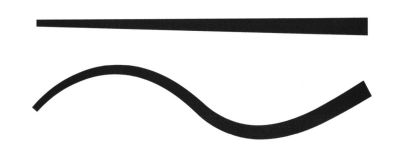

Mild Wedge

Because these brushes are solid black and have their Colorization method set to Tints, you can make them any color you choose by changing the stroke color of the path they are applied to.

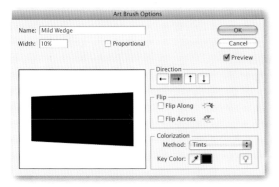

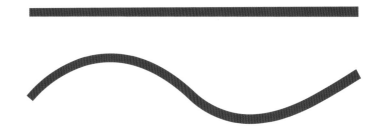

Severe Wedge

The fact that these simple wedge brushes stretch along a path, suits them perfectly because there is no detail to distort.

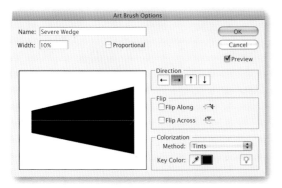

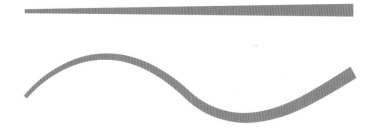

Leaf Branch 1

This rough illustrated leaf will always have a tint fill color because its Colorization method is set to Tints, and the original illustration was black and gray.

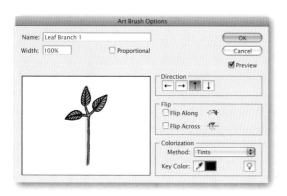

Alstroemeria Stem

This pretty flower brush will grow in proportion to the path it's on.

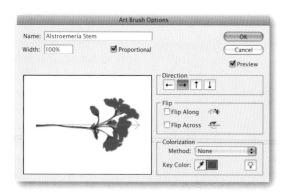

Alstroemeria Single Stem

To change the color of this flower, you have to adapt the original
brush artwork.

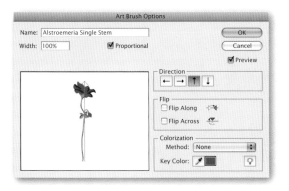

Carnation Stem

No matter which direction you draw in, the head of this flower will always
be at the end of the path, because its Direction is set to upward.

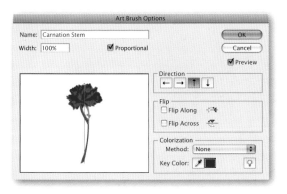

Rose Stem

This rose will grow bigger on longer paths because it is set to Proportional.

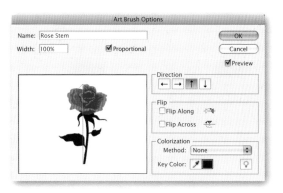

Single Bud Stem

This brush looks great when mixed in with the other Stem brushes.

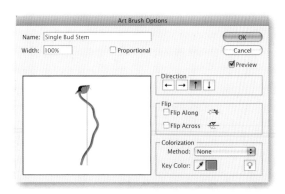

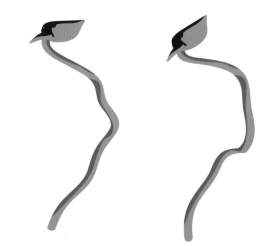

Wild Flower

It doesn't take long to build a whole bunch of flowers with
this busy flower brush.

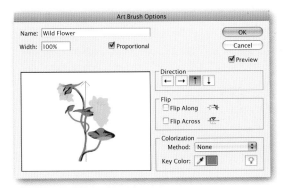

Wild Flower Single Stem

If you want the head of this flower to face the other way,
check the Flip Along box.

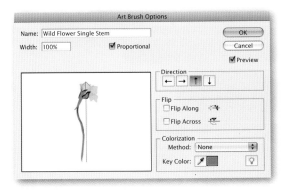

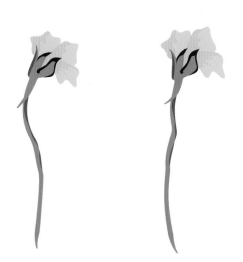

Claw

This spiky Art brush was used in the creation of the Claw font, (see letter C opposite).

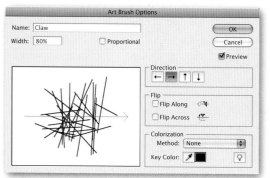

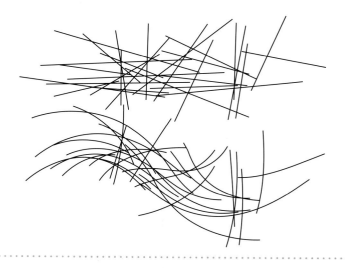

Design: Adam Lewis

Cirkit

This brush makes some great shapes as it distorts on curved paths, and was used in the creation of the Cirkit font (see letter D opposite).

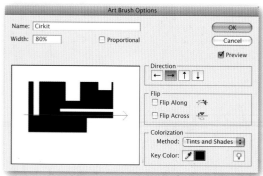

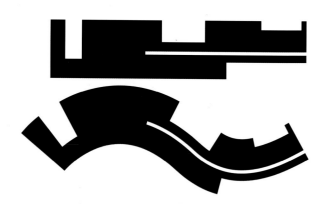

Design: Adam Lewis

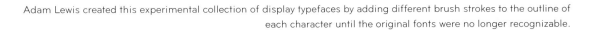

Adam Lewis created this experimental collection of display typefaces by adding different brush strokes to the outline of each character until the original fonts were no longer recognizable.

Wire

This geometric brush was used in the creation of the Wire font
by Adam Lewis (see letter B on the previous page).

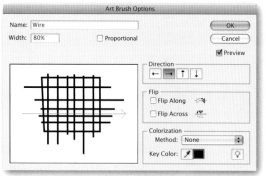

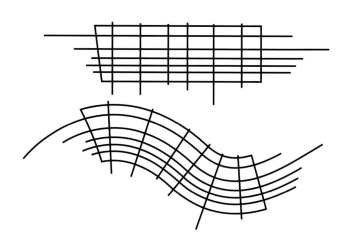

Design: Adam Lewis

Peanut

This unusual shaped brush can give great character to a simple path,
and was used in the creation of the I Hate Football illustration on page 161.

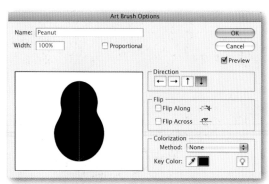

Design: Julian James

154

Streamline

These stripes are great for creating the impression of movement.

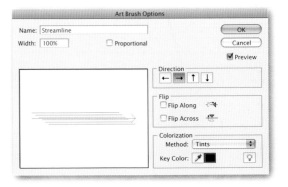

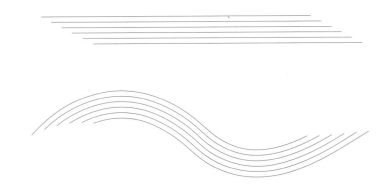

Hand

This hand can reach out forever, and was used in the creation of the I Hate Football illustration on page 161.

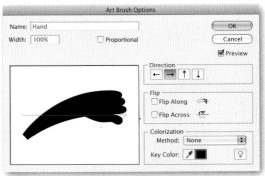

Design: Julian James

Using scale tutorial

The option to have your Art brush grow proportionally on a path means that you can stop the brush stretching and achieve some great scale effects.

Things that grow organically, such as blades of grass, vary in size, so make perfect proportional Art brushes. As do objects that you want to appear in perspective, for example street lamps positioned along a road that disappears into the distance.

The Growing Mountain brush (see page 133) creates a mountain range with perspective.

1. Draw your mountain and fill it with vibrant colors. To create a neat mountain range it is best if your original mountain drawing has a flat bottom edge.

2. Now load your drawing into a new Art brush.

3. In the Art Brush Options window, check the Proportional box.

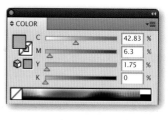

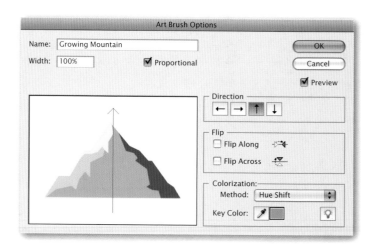

4. You will probably need to change the direction of the brush, since the default direction for Art brushes is set depending on whether or not the original illustration is landscape or portrait format. If your original object is landscape, then the direction will be to the right, and if it's portrait, then it will automatically be downward. In the case of the Growing Mountain brush, the original illustration is landscape format, so the direction will be set to the right, but you want mountains that grow upward, so change the Direction to the up arrow.

5. Although the colors you used for the original mountain drawing were appropriate and you want to retain them, you also want to be able to make the mountains appear fainter in the distance. Change the Colorization method to Hue Shift—this will allow you to subtly change the stroke color of a path, and change the overall hue of the mountain placed on that path.

6. Once you're happy with your options and you've given your brush a name, click OK and you're ready to create your range. Draw a number of lines of various lengths upward. The longer the line, the bigger the mountain. Change the stroke color for each path to create a realistic variant in the hue of the mountains.

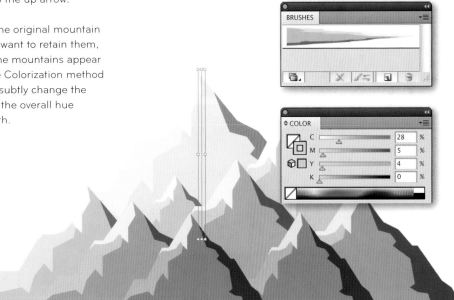

Object repeat tutorial

Scatter and Pattern brushes can duplicate a single image along a path, but what if you want that image to get bigger or smaller as it goes along the path? To achieve this kind of effect, you need to use an Object Blend and an Art brush (see pages 230–233 for more details about Object Blend).

You can Object Blend any image you like, but for the purposes of this tutorial, we're going to use an elephant. From one elephant we're going to make a family of elephants walking in procession, with the baby elephant trailing behind (see page 133 for the brush). If elephants seem a little daunting, you could do the same tutorial with a circle to start you off.

1. Draw your elephant. If you're not great at drawing from memory, you can trace one. Find a picture of an elephant and put it on a template layer underneath your active drawing layer—this way you can work in Outline view (View > Outline, or ⌘ + Y), and still see the image you are tracing.

2. Your illustration can be made up of as many different components as you like. This won't hinder the Object Blend as long as (once you're satisfied with your illustration) you group all the elements together (Object > Group or ⌘ + G).

3. This elephant will be the largest in your procession so scale it accordingly.

4. Select your elephant and duplicate it, by holding down ⇧ (shift) and alt as you drag—this will duplicate your illustration and keep it parallel with the original. Reduce the size of your new elephant to make it the baby.

5. Keeping the elephants parallel, position them a way apart from each other—you can always adjust this distance after you have performed the Object Blend.

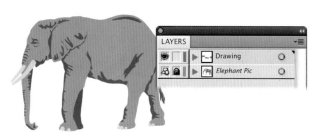

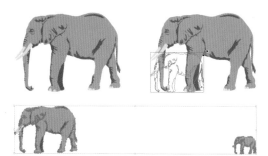

6. Open the Blend Options window: Object > Blend > Blend Options… or double-click the Blend Tool icon. Set the Spacing to Specified Steps, and type in the number of elephants you want to appear between your two original elephants. Click OK.

7. Select both your elephants and blend them together: Object > Blend > Make (alt + apple + B), or use the Blend tool. Not only will the new in-between elephants be positioned from the large elephant to the small one, they will also gradually reduce in size.

8. If the elephants overlap and you don't want them to, you can move the two original elephants further apart which will respace all the elephants in between: double-click on the elephant at either end and move it away.

9. Because the elephants get smaller in size and the spacing between them is consistent, the spaces appear bigger the smaller the elephants get. If you want to reposition the in-between elephants, you'll need to expand the object blend: Object > Blend > Expand and then ungroup the elephants: Ungroup (⇧ + ⌘ + G). Now you can reposition each elephant as you wish.

10. Once you're happy with the position of your elephants, select them all and load them into a new Art brush.

11. In the Art Brush Options window, check the Proportional box, so that your elephants don't become distorted. You shouldn't need to adjust the options for this Art brush.

12. When you've named your brush, click OK. Now your procession of elephants can travel on any path you like.

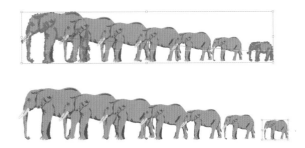

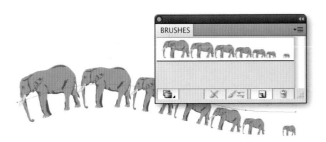

Pattern brushes

5

6

1. **We've Moved by Ben the Illustrator**
Three original brushes were used in the creation of this image: the grass effect, the bunting, and the scene as a whole.

2. **Synergize Vernacular Art and Contemporary project by Saurabh Gupta**
Saurabh designed 25 original Pattern brushes representing contemporary lifestyles to create a modern form of Gond Art (traditional tribal folk art painting of India).

3. **Kitsch fabric swatches by Emily Portnoi**
All the items on these fabric swatches were drawn in the Pattern brushes Sketch Pen 1, 2, and 3.

4. **I Hate Football illustration by Julian James**
This illustration uses a mix of specially-created Art and Pattern brushes.

5. **Seven Star Soccer logo by David Caunce**
The wreath around this shield was created using a modified version of the Laurel Pattern brush (one of the brushes that is built in to the Illustrator program).

6. **Vector Renikx illustration by hellrom**
A special brush set was used to create the hair and eyelashes for this portrait.

4

Pattern brushes explained

Pattern brushes, when built properly, are the toughest to make, but they are by far the most flexible, impressive, and useful of all brushes. Illustrator comes with a few built-in and you can pick up the odd one or two on the internet, but these only scratch the surface of what is possible if you learn to make brushes yourself.

There is a bit more to learn and master with Pattern brushes; rather than starting life as just one illustration, they have five separate sections which apply to different parts of your path. Each section bends to your path, and there are three separate modes for fitting Pattern brushes to your path. However, once you understand a few key rules, you'll be able to use and adapt these rules to make new brushes that work seamlessly.

The Tiles

The first step to mastering Pattern brushes is to understand that they are composed of five different sections, which are called tiles: Side, Inner Corner, Outer Corner, Start, and End. Not all Pattern brushes come complete with all the various tiles; in fact, you only need the side tiles for your Pattern brush to paint.

You can see the various sections of a brush displayed in the Brushes palette when in Thumbnail View. And, although the preview will always look different because it is showing the tiles of a specific brush, the tiles are always displayed in the same order: Outer Corner, Side, Inner Corner, Start, and End.

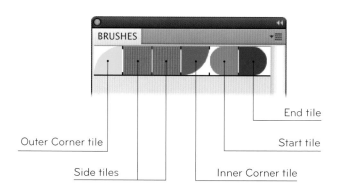

Making a Pattern brush—swatches

The process of making a new Pattern brush starts in exactly the same way as making a new Art or Scatter brush, the only difference being that you need to make a maximum of five illustrations, which will become your five tiles.

For the purpose of mastering Pattern brushes, keep your first brush simple—make all your tiles square, but color them differently so that you can easily identify them.

Now that you have five tile illustrations, you need to turn them into Pattern brush tiles, and, as usual, there is more than one way to do this.

1. Making tiles through the Swatches palette

Drag each individual tile into your Swatches palette. Once you have dragged a tile in, double-click on it and give it a name (naming each tile will help you to find the right one when you are building your brush).

When all your tiles are loaded into the Color palette and named, either:

1. **Click the New Brush icon** at the bottom of your brushes palette, or

2. **Select New Brush from** the Brushes palette menu.

Either action will bring up the New Brush window. Select New Pattern Brush and then OK.

1.

2.

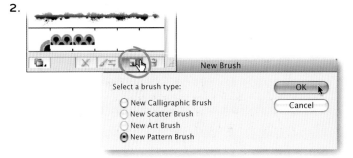

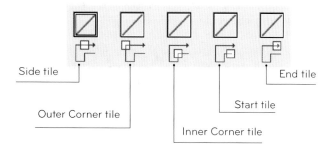

Side tile

Outer Corner tile

Inner Corner tile

Start tile

End tile

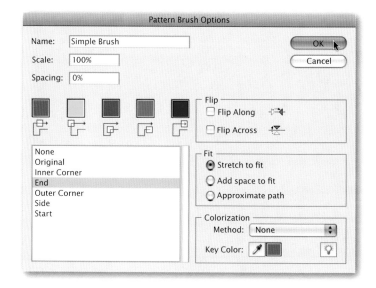

This will open the Pattern Brush Options window. You'll see that there are five empty spaces for your tiles, with a diagram under each one to tell you which tile should go where. Confusingly, these don't appear in the same order as they do in the Brushes palette preview.

Below the empty spaces is a window with a list of all the swatches in your palette. All the names you gave your tiles should be in this list. All you have to do is select the appropriate name from the list to go in each of the empty spaces.

Once all the spaces have been filled, name your brush and click OK. Your new Pattern brush will now appear in your Brushes palette.

Tip: The same method can also be used to replace existing tiles.

Tip: Once your brush is complete you can delete the tiles from your Swatches palette if you wish—it will have no effect on your brush.

Making a Pattern brush—dragging

2. Making tiles by dragging and dropping

You can also load your tiles into a new (or existing) Pattern brush by dragging and dropping them into the Brushes palette, in the same way as you do for Scatter or Art Brushes.

Drag your Side tile artwork from the artboard into your Brushes palette (you have to start off with your Side tile). The New Brush window will appear. Select New Pattern Brush and then OK.

When the Pattern Brush Options window opens, you'll see that the space for the Side tile has been filled, but all the rest are empty. The name "Original" will have been added to the list of swatches below.

Name your brush and click OK.

Your new brush will be in your Brushes palette, but as yet it will only have Side tiles.

To add more tiles to your brush, select the tile artwork you want, and drag it from the artboard into the relevant space on the preview in your Brushes palette, while holding down the alt key.

The Pattern Brush Options window will appear again, with your new tile in place. Click OK.

Repeat the process until you have filled all the tile spaces you want for that brush.

Tip: The same method of dragging a tile onto the brush preview in your Brushes palette, while holding down alt, can also be used to replace existing tiles.

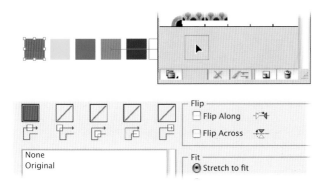

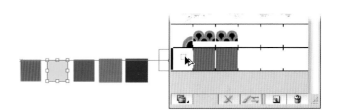

Pattern Brush Options

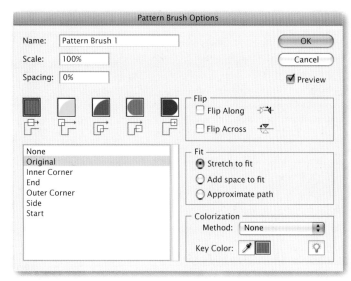

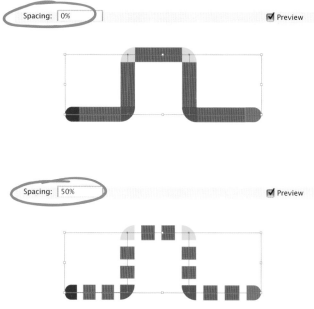

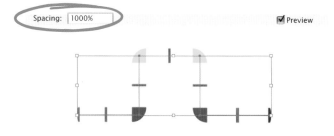

As with the other types of brushes, the Pattern Brush Options window houses a number of variable settings to customize your brush.

Scale adjusts the size of the brush relative to your original tile size, it can be anything from 1% to 10,000%.

Spacing adjusts the space between tiles. The default setting for this is 0%, which means no space between the tiles. This can be adjusted from 0% to 10,000%. You can't make tiles overlap by having negative space between them.

Flip: these two options can change the direction of your brush on a path.

- **Flip Along** flips your brush horizontally on your path, so your start tile will be placed at the end of your path, your end tile will be placed at the beginning, and all the tiles in between will be reversed.

- **Flip Across** flips your brush vertically on your path, so your inner corner tile will be placed at your outer corners, and your outer corner tile will be placed at your inner corners.

Fit: there are three fit options, the default is Stretch to fit.

- **Stretch to fit** is the default fit options it shrinks or stretches tiles to make them fit to your path. This can cause distortion.

- **Add space to fit** adds space between the tiles to make them fit to your path without distorting the tiles. This means that your tiles are likely not to meet.

- **Approximate path** places the number of tiles on your path which closest matches your path without distorting the tiles or adding space. This option normally results in your shape being slightly bigger or smaller than your original path.

Colorization is covered on pages 20 to 21.

Preview will show you how your settings will affect your brush on any existing path it is applied to.

Aligning edges: key rules

1. **When possible, make all your tiles the same height, and make your Corner tiles square.**

Side, Start, and End tiles fit side by side on a path, with vertical edge touching vertical edge, even when traveling on a vertical path. Corner tiles meet other tiles on their vertical and horizontal edges. So the easiest way to make tiles that are guaranteed to fit together is to make all your tiles the same height, and make your corner tiles square.

2. **Know which edges of which tiles are going to meet.**

When you're designing a complicated brush, it's important to know which edges are going to meet.

The diagram below shows which edges will meet. To make sure every possible combination of touching edges join together seamlessly, you can only have two edge designs and they must fit together—in the case of the example, the tip of the triangle and the base of the triangle.

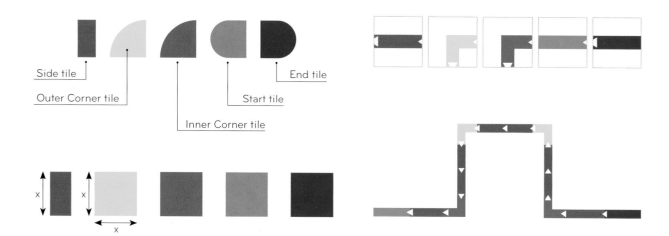

Side tile

Outer Corner tile

Inner Corner tile

Start tile

End tile

3. **Remember that tiles always align by their central horizontal axes, regardless of their design or height.**

If you are designing a slightly more complicated Pattern brush, your tiles may have varying heights, so the top and bottom edges of your tiles won't align. If this doesn't suit your design, then you will need to add some empty space to ensure that the tile designs meet in the position you want them to.

Align your tiles as you want them to meet, and then create boxes of equal height to contain each tile (make sure your boxes are not wider than your tile design). These boxes need no fill or stroke, but must be imported with the design as part of the tile.

4. **Tiles must be horizontal to make a brush.**

You can design tiles any which way you like, but before loading them into a brush you must make sure they are horizontal.

It doesn't matter if you design the tiles all vertically, they still won't rotate when they become a brush.

Once your brush is made you can apply it to any direction of path.

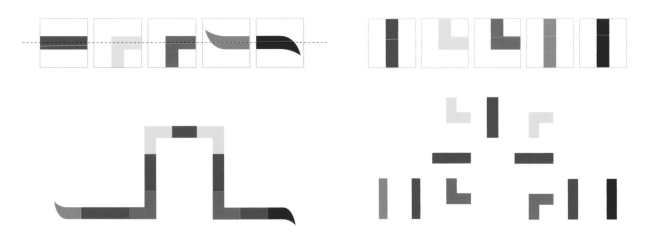

Corner tiles: key rules

Of all the tiles, Corners can give you the most problems. Here are a few rules to help you tame them.

1. Both Corner tiles must always start life as upper right-hand Outer Corners.

It is not the angle you design them at, but the tile slot that you put them in, that will determine whether or not they are an Outer Corner tile or an Inner Corner tile.

If you make your corner tiles as upper right outer corners, you can apply that tile design to both the Outer Corner tile slot and the Inner Corner tile slot, and it will fit any path perfectly. If you design your corner tiles based on any other corner, for example bottom left outer corner, then they won't fit to your path.

You'll notice that once you load your corner tile design into the inner corner tile slot, it will appear rotated in the Brushes palette preview.

You can design your corner tiles specifically to be Inner Corner or Outer Corner, but they still need to be at the same angle.

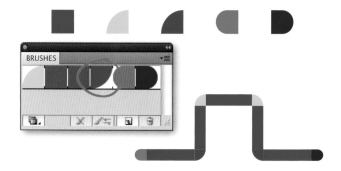

Both Corner tiles designed as upper right corners, will work

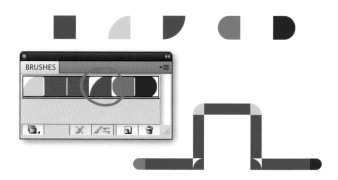

Outer Corner tile design as upper right corner, and Inner Corner tile designed as a lower left corner, won't work

2. Corner tiles must have a square frame.

Because corner tiles meet the other tiles on both their horizontal and vertical edges, all four sides need to be equal.

This doesn't mean that all corner tiles designs have to actually be square, but they should have a square frame. The square frame does not need to have any stroke or fill color, but it must be imported as part of your tile design.

To ensure your corner tile's frame is the correct size, duplicate your Side tile and rotate it 90° counterclockwise. You won't use this rotated Side tile as part of your final brush, only to help with the design of your corner tile.

Draw guides along the top and bottom of the horizontal Side tile, and up from the sides of the verticle Side tile.

Now draw a square where the guides intersect. This square can either be your corner tile's design or it can be the frame which contains your corner tile design.

When you've created your corner tile designs, you can add them to a brush, ensuring that the square frame is part of the final tile.

You can see if your brush tiles are going to align in the Brushes palette preview.

The only time when you would ignore this rule is if you didn't want your corner tiles to align.

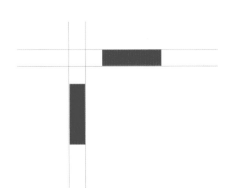

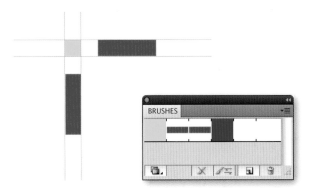

Teardrop Leaf

This pretty border brush has a different design for its inner and outer corner tiles.

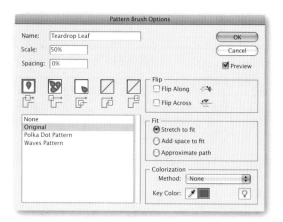

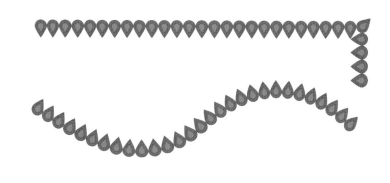

Blue Shells

Its well-crafted corner pieces make this brush great for creating borders.

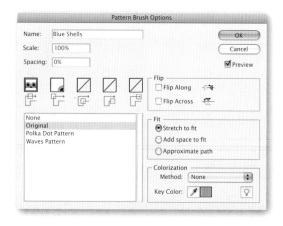

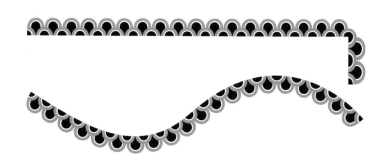

1950s Trim

A great border brush which takes you right back to the
days of Formica tables and Stepford housewives.

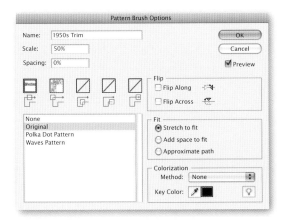

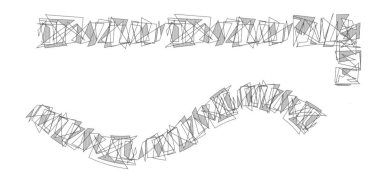

Safari

This brush's corner was created by using a Side tile only brush to draw a curved corner square.
The corners of the square were then isolated and expanded to form the corner tiles of the final brush.

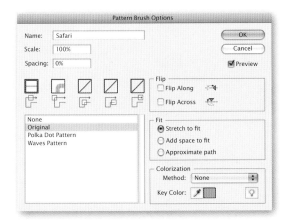

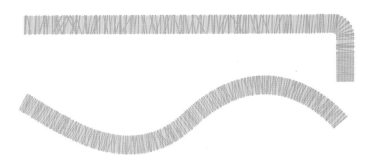

Ocean Swirls

This brush is quite large and detailed, so when your path has sides shorter than the length of the Side tiles of the brush, the sides overlap the corners to give a wonderfully dramatic frame.

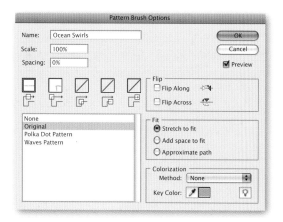

Golden Swirls

This brush started life as an ink drawing and was scanned and vectorized using the Live Trace feature in Illustrator. The level of detail applied in Live Trace means it has retained its hand-drawn quality.

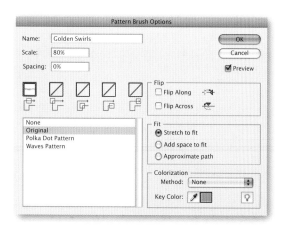

Basic Scales

This brush was used in the creation of the Loch Ness Monster brush on page 182.

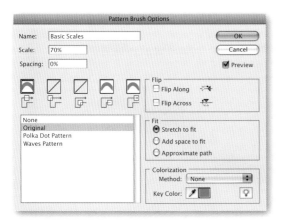

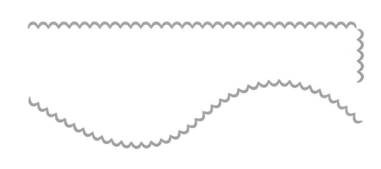

Colored Scales

When applied to paths that sit close together, this brush creates a surface of overlapping scales.

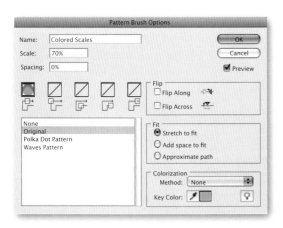

Splatter Paintbrush 1

A great messy Pattern brush, its Colorization method is set to Hue Shift, so you can make the paint whatever color you like by changing the stroke color of the path it is applied to.

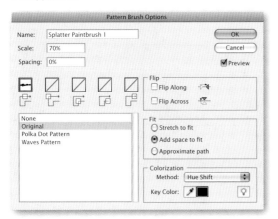

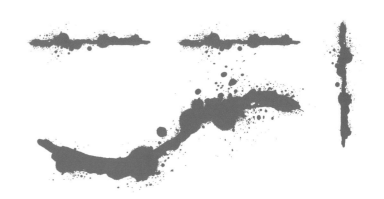

Splatter Paintbrush 2

Try combining Splatter Paintbrush 1 and 2 for a more random and realistic paint effect.

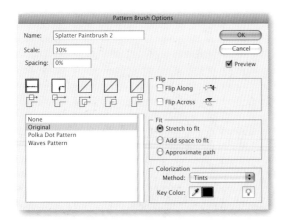

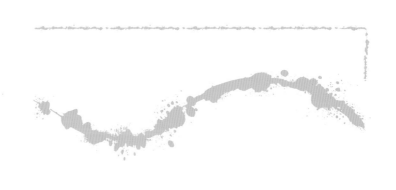

Paint Splatter 1

This border splatter brush is great for creating arts-and-crafts graphics.

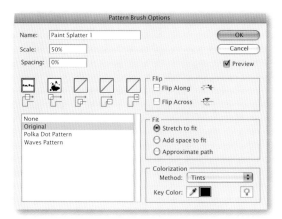

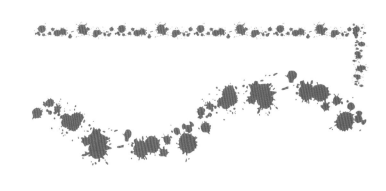

Paint Splatter 2

Create a giant splatter by drawing a filled shape with this brush, and making the fill and stroke the same color.

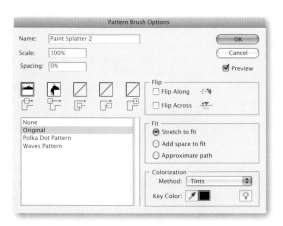

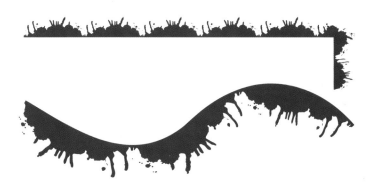

Basic Growing Tree

This brush only has a Side tile and an End tile. The Side tile is the trunk of the tree and the End tile is the foliage, so your tree can be as tall as you like, without its shape ever distorting.

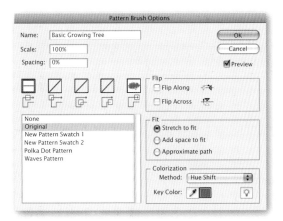

Complex Growing Tree

The leaves on this tree were created using a leaf design Scatter brush. By adjusting the Scale and Rotation settings and the stroke color of the leaf Scatter brush, it was possible to build up realistic-looking foliage.

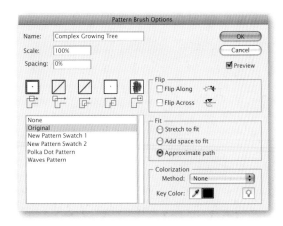

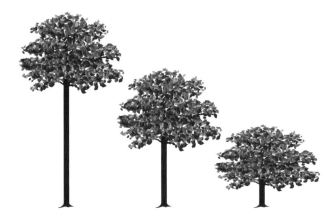

Paint Drip

This brush has a Start, Side, and End tile. The Side tile will duplicate itself, so the longer your path the longer the drip.

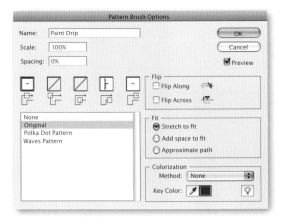

Growing Coin Stack

Each tile of this brush had to be loaded into the brush vertically, even though eventually you would want them to sit horizontally on a vertical path.

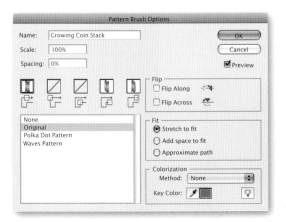

179

Growing High-Rise 1 & 2

Both these buildings can be as tall as you like, and they will never distort.

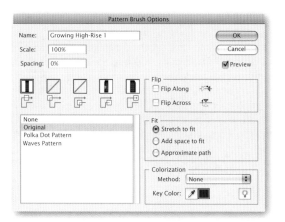

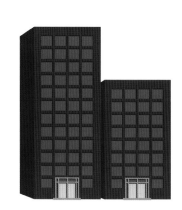

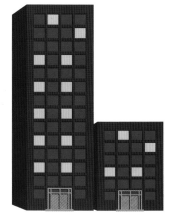

Angled Growing High-Rise 1 & 2

When designing these Angled Growing High-Rise brushes, making sure each tile met the next exactly was critical.

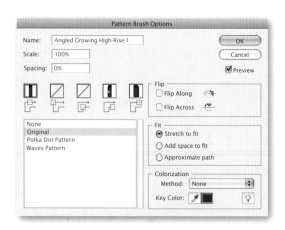

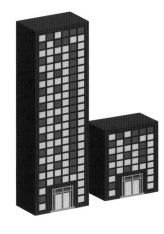

Short Piped Frosting & Long Piped Frosting

The shorter of these two brushes has a short Side tile, so the detail will not become squashed on a short path.

The longer brush has a long Side tile with more detail, so provides more variation on longer paths.

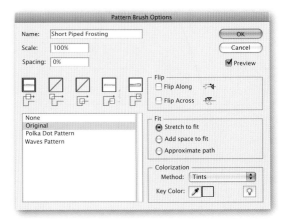

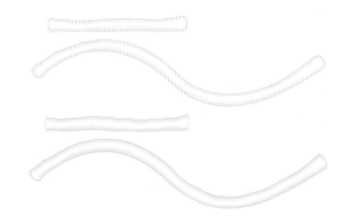

Cartoon Bubble 1 & 2

Both these brushes make great speech bubbles, clouds, or bouncing lines.

The varying thickness of the lines was created by drawing with a tapered Art brush.

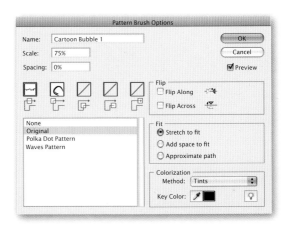

Growing Needle and Thread

No matter how long your thread, your needle will never stretch. A good tip for using this brush is to make sure the first two anchor points have a straight path between them; this way your needle will stay straight.

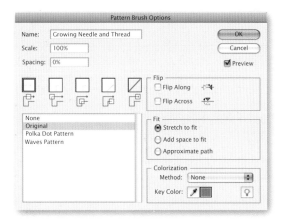

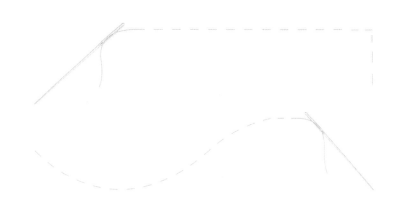

Loch Ness Monster

This growing brush can be as long as you like, without ever distorting, because the Side tile will repeat to fit the path.

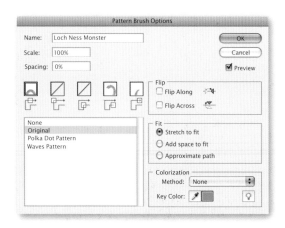

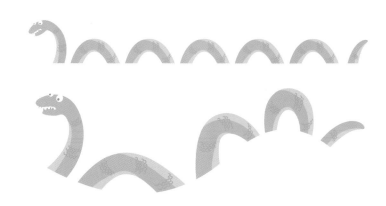

The art of the indigenous Gond community of central India is figurative work rich in colors. Saurabh Gupta wanted to enable this art to be practiced digitally and applied in new ways so that it could reach a wider audience. He collaborated with several artists from the Gond community, and interpreted the visual styles as Illustrator brushes. The brushes were then combined and applied to textiles and stationery.

Car Tire Tracks

The corners of this Pattern brush had to be curved to replicate the way a car turns.

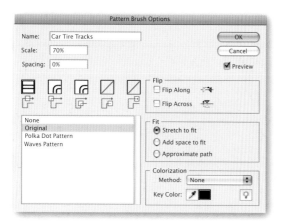

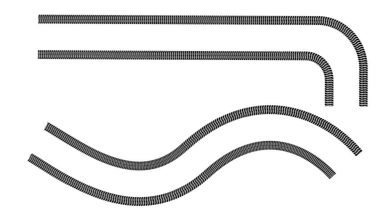

Motorbike Tire Tracks

With this type of brush you have to pay special attention to which edges of which tiles are going to meet, and make sure that the pattern of the tire joins perfectly.

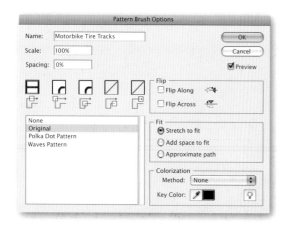

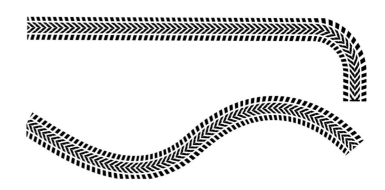

Footprints

The Side tile of this brush doesn't feature a full print, so one footprint will always slightly overlap the position of the last.

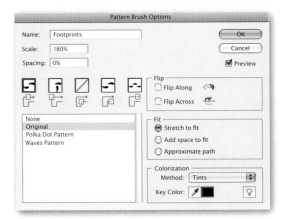

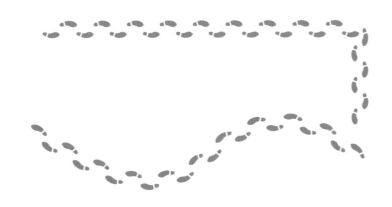

Animal Tracks

The tiles for this brush contain a lot of empty space to ensure that the tracks are evenly spaced out.

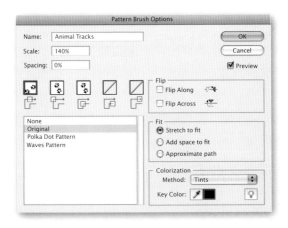

Vine

Whether it's up the side of a house, or the side of a page, this vine can grow and grow without stretching the leaf detail.

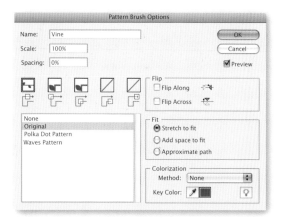

Budding Vine

If you want to change the color of the buds, but keep the leaves the same green, then you will have to adapt the original brush artwork.

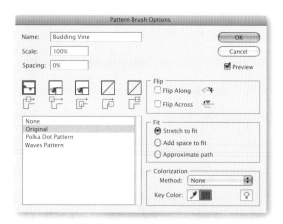

Spiky Grass

This simple grass brush can be any shade of green you like, because its Colorization method is set to Tints.

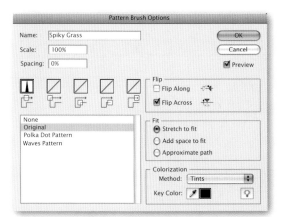

Design: Julian James

Foliage

Unlike the similar Art brush, it doesn't matter how long a path you apply this brush to—the leaf at the end will never stretch.

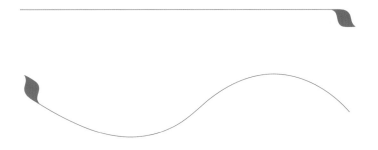

Arrows

For arrows that follow a path, you can use an orderly Scatter brush, but if you want them to curve with the path they are on, then you need a Pattern brush.

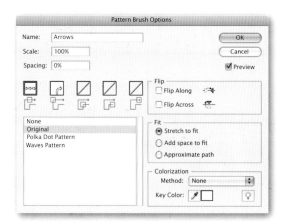

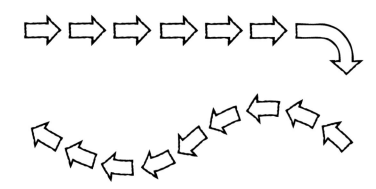

Shadow Arrows

These arrows have a built-in drop shadow, which gives them a comic-book feel.

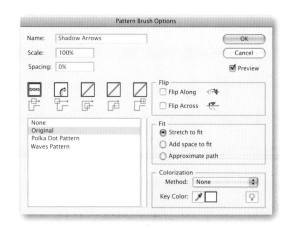

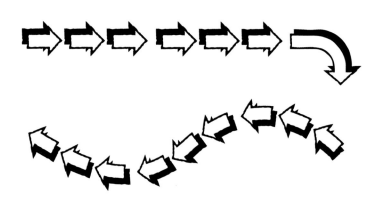

Printed Arrow

With this brush it doesn't matter that the end tile is taller than all the others, because they all align horizontally.

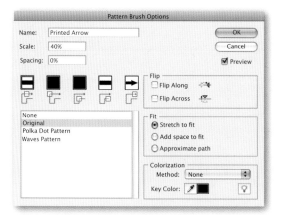

Print Arrows 2

Unlike the similar Arrows Scatter brush, these arrows will bend themselves around a curved path,

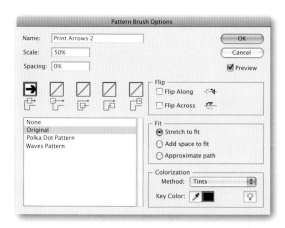

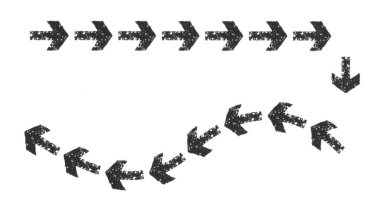

Grass 1

This repeat grass Pattern brush was used in the creation of the
Do The Whirlwind illustration on page 9.

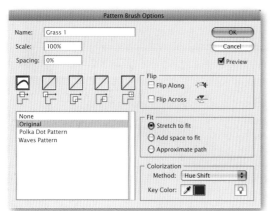

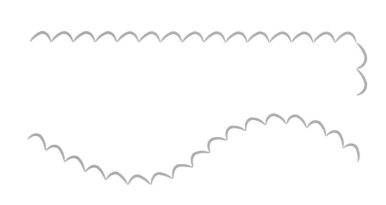

Design: Ben O'Brien

Grass 2

This original brush was created for the We've Moved illustration on page 160.
Its Colorization method is set to Hue Shift, so you can dictate the color with your stroke color.

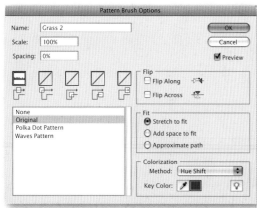

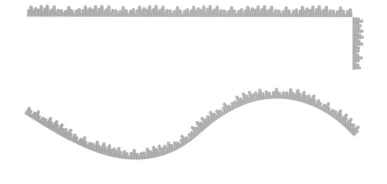

Design: Ben O'Brien

Leaves

These leaves blow in the wind of the Do The Whirlwind illustration on page 9.

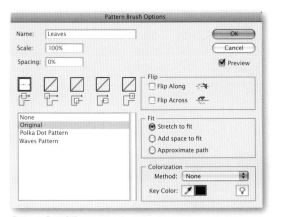

Design: Ben O'Brien

Growing Leaf Branch

This stem can grow to any lengths without ever stretching the leaves at the end.

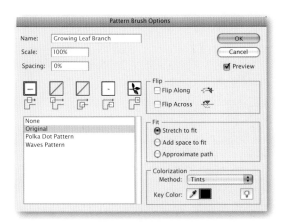

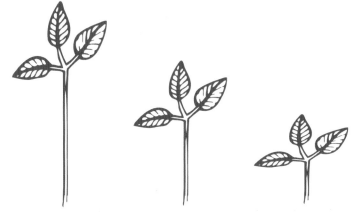

Pine Frame & Walnut Frame

These two detailed frame brushes were shaded with an Object Blend, one to look like pine, and the other to look like walnut.

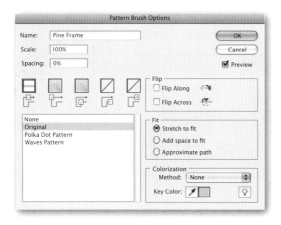

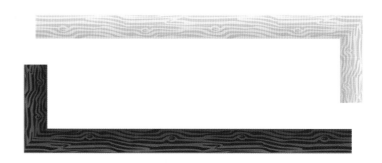

Frame Chevron 1

These frame chevrons were designed to slightly overlap any path they sit on, by adding empty space to the corner tiles.

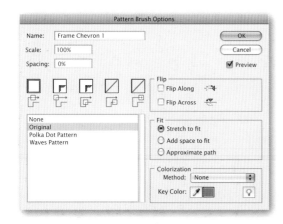

Frame Chevron 2

These cartoon frame chevrons are red and gold, but if you want to change the
color, you can either adapt the original artwork or change the Colorization method.

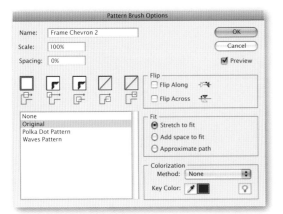

Frame Chevron 3

All the Frame Chevron brushes are corner-only brushes and were
created with invisible Side tiles.

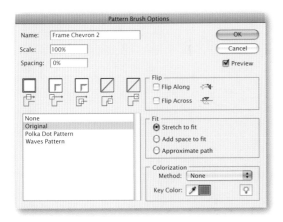

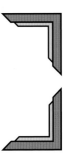

Molecules

This simple and scientifically-themed brush makes a great straightforward border, but change the Colorization method, and it also works beautifully in free-flowing illustrations.

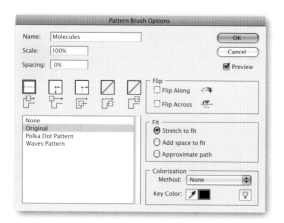

Fur Edge

This fur trim was used in the creation of the Bunnies Scatter brush on page 76.

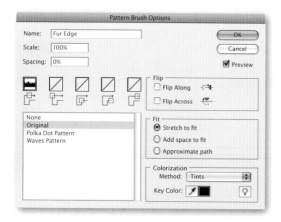

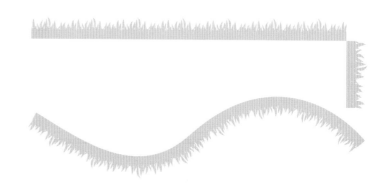

Waves

These surfer waves have a rippled edge because they were Live Traced from a hand-drawn sketch.

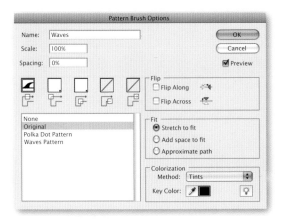

···

Ripple

There will never be any gaps between the Side tiles of this brush because its Fit option is set to Stretch to fit.

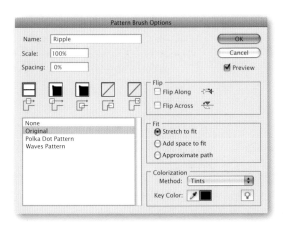

Star Burst

These star burst petals will always fade to white no matter what color you make them, because their Colorization method is set to Tints, which doesn't affect white in the original brush artwork.

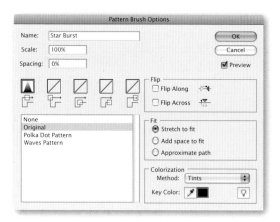

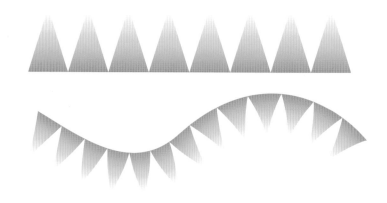

Spikes

The base of these spikes will always sit flush with any path they are applied to, because there is extra empty space in the Side tile.

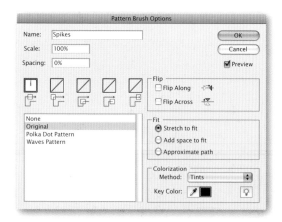

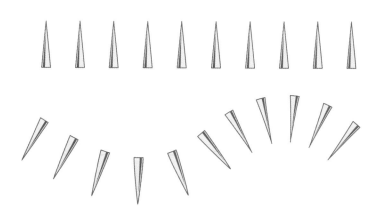

Country Detail 1 & 2

Country Detail 1 is outlines only; Country Detail 2 has different shades of gray in the original
artwork, which will become shades of whatever stroke color you set in your color palette.

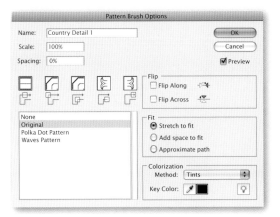

Bunting

This pastel bunting is great for party invites, and because it
has a simple corner tile, you can hang it any way you like.

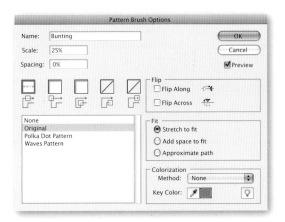

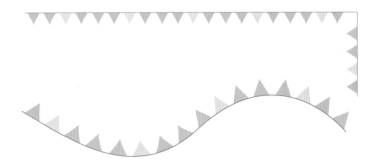

Wobbly Pencil

This brush started life as a pencil drawing on a rough piece of card and was transformed into a vector illustration using Live Trace.

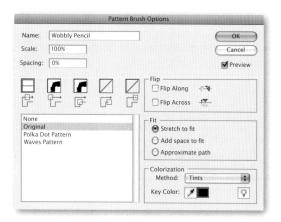

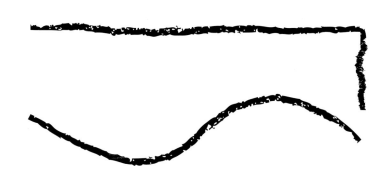

Straight Pencil

The very rough texture of this brush means that the Side tiles don't have to join perfectly for the brush to look realistic.

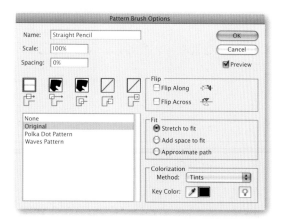

Wobbly Line

This brush was used in the creation of the Slanted Arrows Scatter brush on page 81.

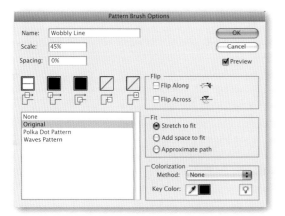

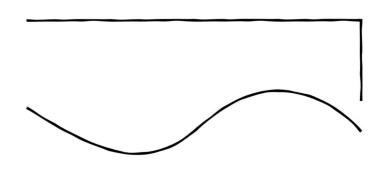

Dashed Sketch Pen

Great for a hand-drawn diagram look, which you can see used on page 32.

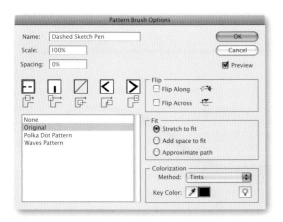

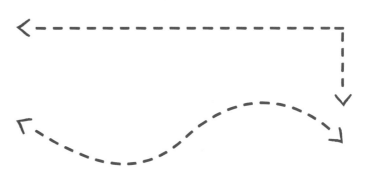

Emboss

This emboss effect brush was used in the creation of the Photo
Corners brushes on page 210, and was made using an Object Blend.

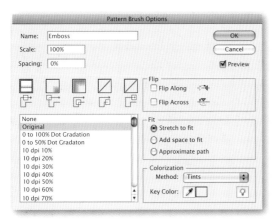

Sketch Pen 1

This brush's side tiles don't join flush, which gives the
impression of sketching using lots of short lines.

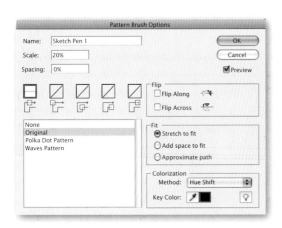

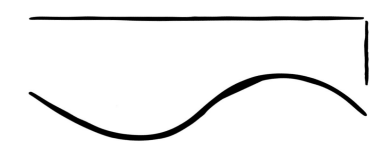

Sketch Pen 2

This sketch pen has a longer Side tile with more detail, so your drawings will have a more natural variation on long paths.

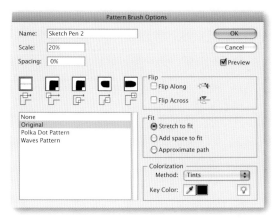

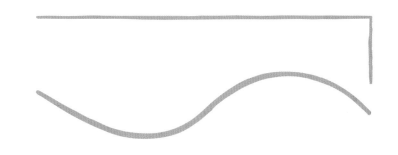

Sketch Pen 3

This sketch pen has a shorter Side tile, so won't become compressed on shorter paths.

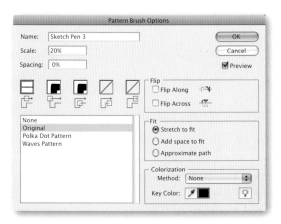

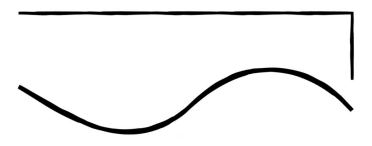

Swirl Border

This swirly border was created using a daub-shaped Art brush.

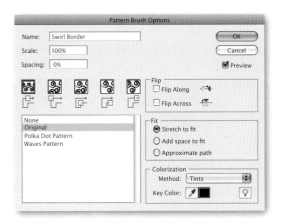

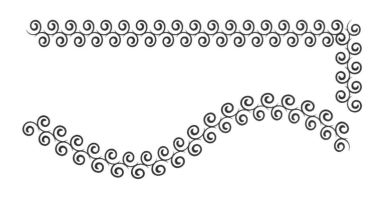

Swirl Stem

The swirl detail at the end of this brush will never stretch,
no matter how long a path it is applied to.

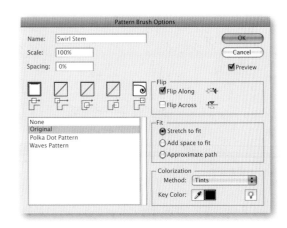

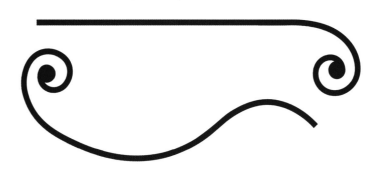

Growing Leaf Stem 1

This brush can add simple rococo detail to a design.

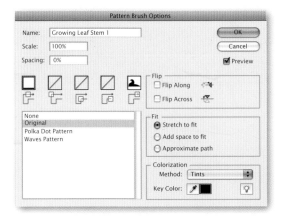

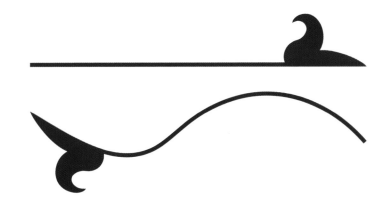

Arabesque

This detailed border brush aligns seamlessly, even on corners.

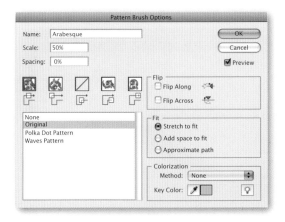

Suspension Bridge

Sometimes a Side tile is all you need—as is the case with this simple industrial brush.

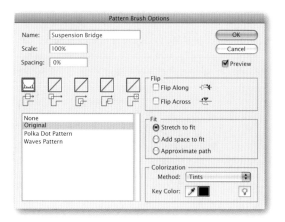

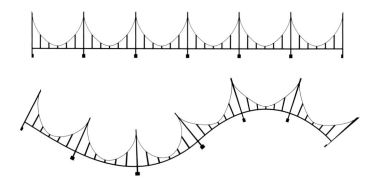

Road

Create giant interchanges within seconds with this simple Road brush.

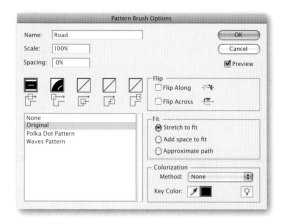

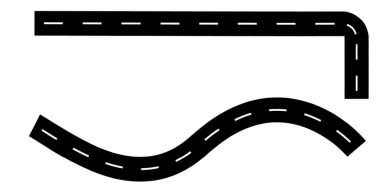

Shoe Lace

You can make this lace any color you choose by changing the stroke color, but the shading will always remain, to add depth and detail to the brush.

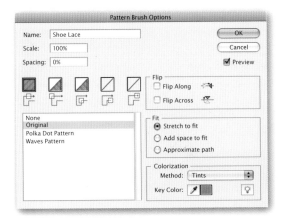

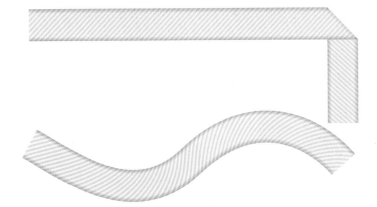

Cotton Thread

This very detailed brush has all five tiles, so can do anything you ask of it.

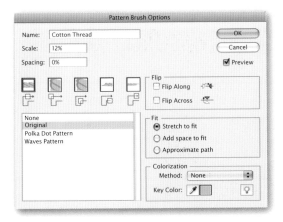

Flowing Ribbon

A streamer-like ribbon that ripples around corners.

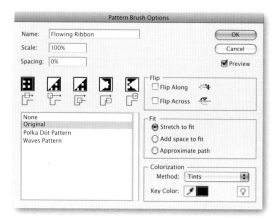

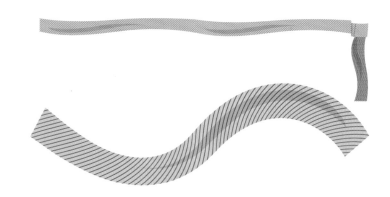

Gingham Ribbon

This detailed ribbon brush folds at the corners and dovetails at both ends.

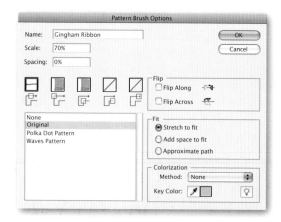

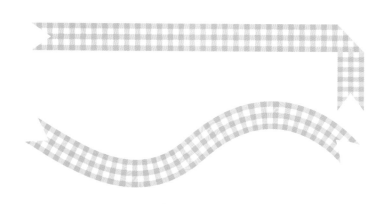

Straight Ribbon

This ribbon is full of detail, from its folded corners to its stitched edges.

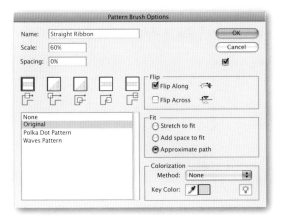

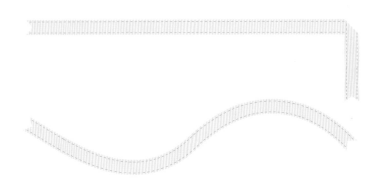

Waved Ribbon

Because of the waving Side tiles, this brush can't have simple square corners; instead it must have straight line corners.

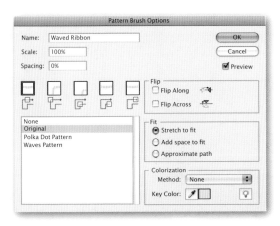

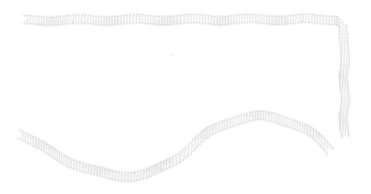

Hand

This clean graphic hand will point in whatever direction you draw your path.

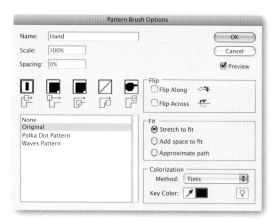

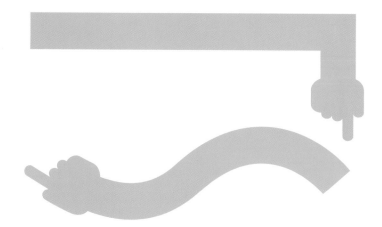

Hands

Wrap your arms around anything you like with this handy brush.

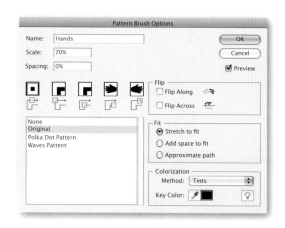

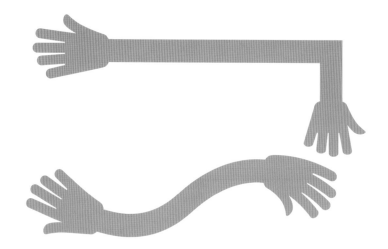

Manicule 1

These two brushes are adapted from manicule punctuation marks, which, though rare today, were commonly used from the 12th to 18th centuries in the margins of books.

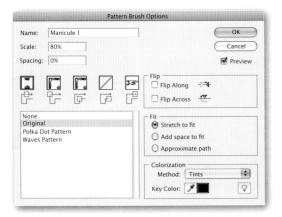

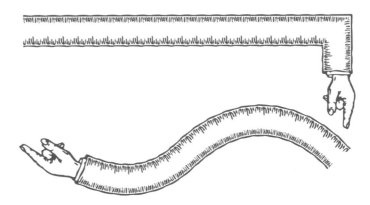

Manicule 2

The hand will always be at the end of any path you draw, but if you want it to be at the beginning, check the Flip Along box.

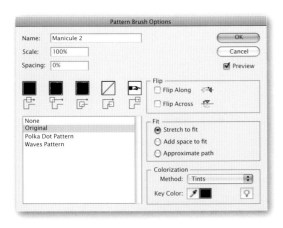

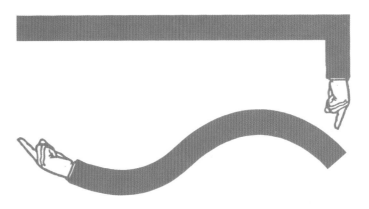

Photo Corners 1

This brush is wonderful for creating a vintage photo album.

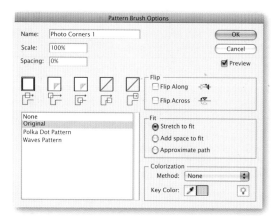

Photo Corners 2

Even though you'll never see the Side tiles of these Photo Corner brushes, they had to be included in the making of this brush because you can't make a Pattern brush without Side tiles.

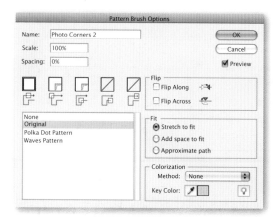

This vintage photo album look was achieved using Photo Corners 1 and 2.

Ornamental Printed Corners

These beautiful woodblock-effect corners can be any color you choose.

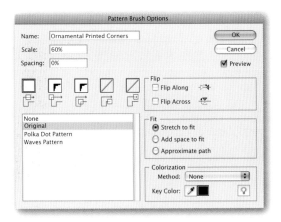

Woodblock Corners

This brush is perfect for making your own digital stamps.

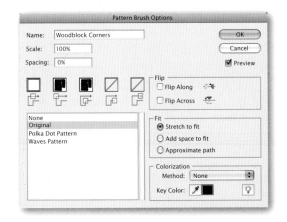

Large Printed Corners

The added empty space in the corner tiles of this brush means that the corners slightly overlap the path they sit on.

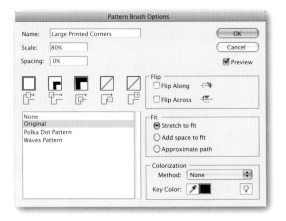

Light Printed Corners

These printed corners mimic the effect of ink running out.

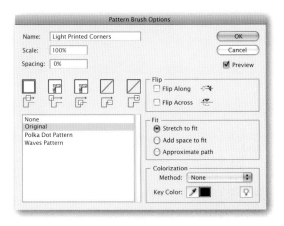

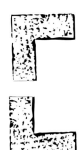

Short Letterpress

This letterpress-effect brush is perfect for short paths because the Side tile will not need to compress.

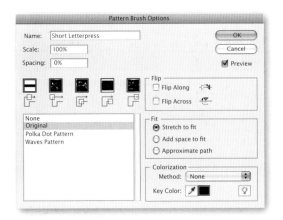

Long Letterpress

This brush has a longer Side tile with more detail, so it doesn't create an obvious repeat pattern when applied to a long path.

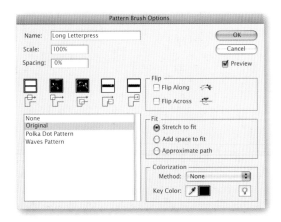

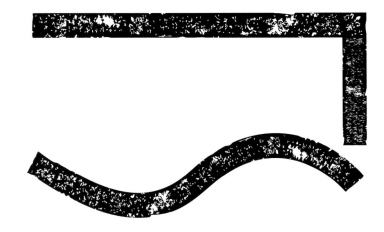

Pearls with Clasp

Because the Side tile is a single pearl and the clasp is the End tile, no matter how long your string of pearls, you will only ever have one clasp on a path.

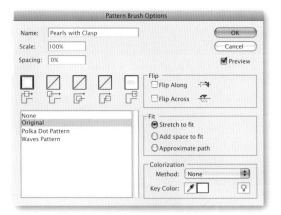

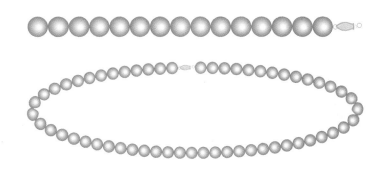

Pearls with Clasp Tints

Because this brush has its Colorization method set to Tints, you can make these pearls any shade you choose, but the clasp will change color too.

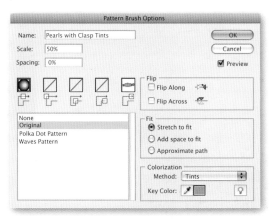

Stripes

This simple brush was created using curved corners.

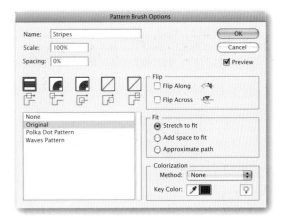

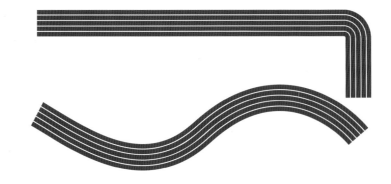

Colored Stripes

Because of the different colored bars, this brush had to have two separate designs for the Inner and Outer Corner tiles.

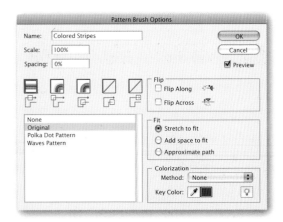

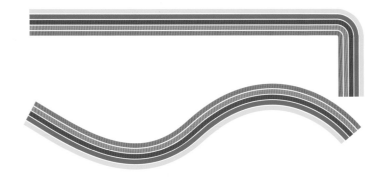

Tapered Stripes

You can change the color of these stripes by altering the original brush artwork or changing the brush's Colorization method.

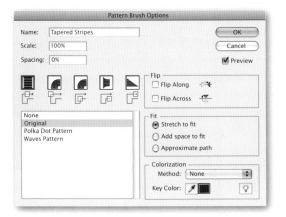

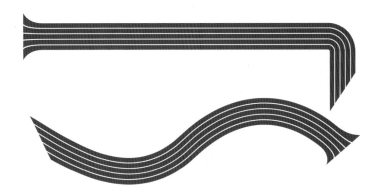

Tapered Colored Stripes

The flared start and chiseled end of this brush give it a 1970s retro feel.

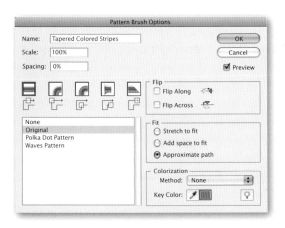

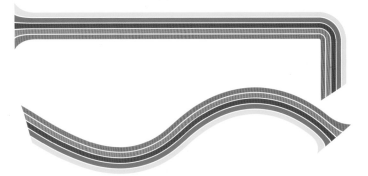

Scene

This beautifully detailed brush features Pattern brush Grass 2 from page 190.

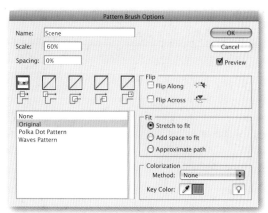

Design: Ilias Sounas

Dream Speakers

One of many brushes which featured in the Follow Your Dreams illustration on page 52.

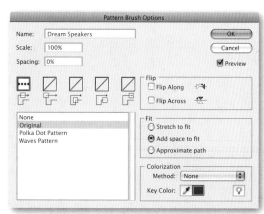

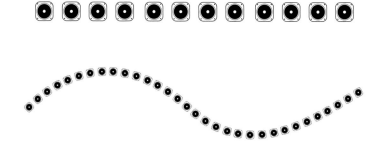

Design: Ilias Sounas

Growing Ionic Column

This column is full of detail, so while it make impressive illustrations, it also makes big files.

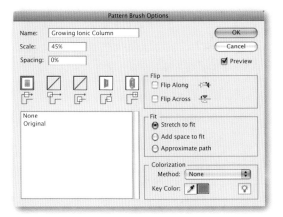

Growing Doric Column

These brushes won't turn corners but they can grow as tall as you like, without ever distorting the top and bottom details.

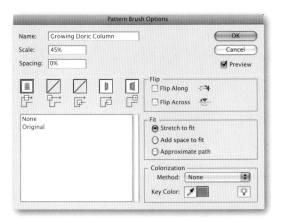

Adding space tutorial

Tiles always align by their central horizontal axes. This is fine if all your tiles are the same height, or they naturally align centrally, but for the occasions when your tiles vary in height and don't align, you'll need to add space using frames.

The Complex Growing Tree Pattern brush (see page 178), is a good example of a brush that doesn't naturally align.

1. For this brush you only need three tiles: Start, End, and Side. The Start will be the branches of the tree, the End will be the roots and the Side will be the trunk. When drawing your tiles make sure your trunk is the same width at both ends, so that you won't see a repeat, when it repeats on a path.

2. Once all three of your tiles are drawn, group all the elements within each tile: Object > Group (⌘ + G) to make sure nothing gets nudged out of place.

3. Align each tile by the part of the brush that will meet. Use the ruler and guides to help you.

4. Draw a rectangle over the tallest tile (in this case the End tile) making sure it encompasses the whole height, but is not wider than the tile artwork—you don't want to add empty space between your tiles. This rectangle is your frame and should have no stroke or fill color.

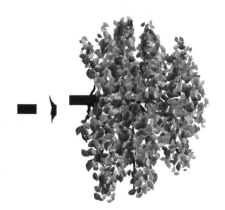

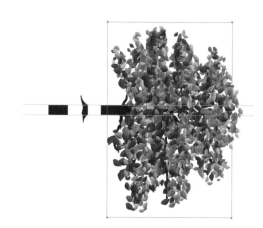

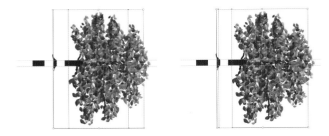

5. Drag the frame over the next tile design while holding down ⇧ (shift) + alt. This will duplicate your frame and keep it parallel with the original.

6. Adjust the width of the new frame to make sure it is not wider than the tile design. But don't change the height.

7. Repeat steps 3 and 4 for your last tile.

8. Now create a Pattern brush using your three tiles, remembering to import the frame with each tile.

Tip:

Because the Complex Growing Tree brush doesn't have any corners, it is not necessary to make any of your frames square. The crucial things to remember are: ensure the frames are all the same height and that they have no stroke or fill color when you import them into your brush.

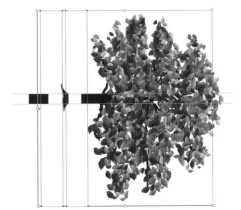

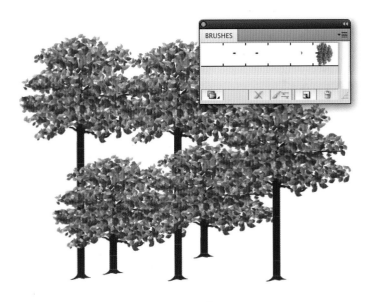

Straight corners tutorial

When your Corner tiles are square and your Sides are square or rectangular, they fit together simply. But not all Corner tiles can be square. If your Side tile design varies in width, then your Corner tile will need to have the appearance of a corner—two sides intersecting. If this is the case, then there are two easy ways to go about creating corners that will perfectly align to the other tiles. The first, a straight line corner, is used in the Molecules Pattern brush (see page 194).

Because the Side tile of the Molecules brush consists of a thin line with wider circles on, its corner tile can't be a simple square.

1. Start by designing your Side tile. Once you're satisfied it's finished, group all the elements within the design: Object > Group (⌘ + G).

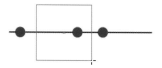

2. Draw a square frame over your Side tile design (to draw a square frame hold down ⇧ [shift] when dragging out the rectangle tool). Make sure the frame encompasses the total height of the design but not the total length and has no stroke or fill color (for the purposes of this tutorial the frames are shown with a pink keyline).

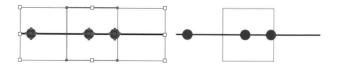

3. Move the frame so that it is horizontally in the middle of your Side tile artwork.

4. Drag the frame and Side tile artwork to the left while holding down ⇧ (shift) + alt. This will duplicate your tile and keep it parallel with the original. This new tile will be your Outer Corner tile.

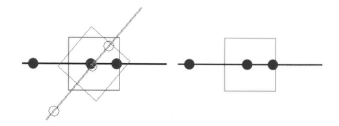

5. Copy and paste the corner frame and artwork in place (⌘ + C, ⌘ + F), and rotate the duplicate 90° counterclockwise around a central point. Select all the elements of the outer corner tile and ungroup them: Object > Ungroup (⇧ + ⌘ + G).

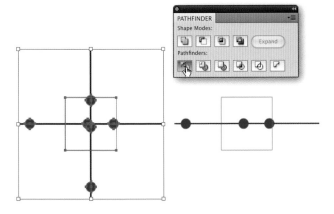

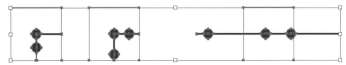

9. Select all the elements of your Outer Corner tile, and drag them to the left while holding down alt—this will duplicate your corner tile.

10. Rearrange the red dots on this duplicated corner tile to make your Inner Corner tile.

11. Now create a new Pattern brush using your three tiles. Don't forget to include the frames when you import the artwork for each tile, and make sure they have no stroke or fill color.

12. When you draw with your new Pattern brush, the corners should align perfectly with the sides.

6. Select the top frame (there will be one on top of another), and the two blue lines. Use the Pathfinders: Divide effect. The Pathfinder effects always leave items grouped, so you'll need to ungroup them again afterward.

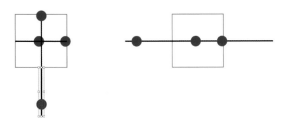

7. Remove all the elements that fall outside of the frame, and the top and left-hand pieces of blue line within the frame. You now have your basic straight line corner.

8. Rearrange the red dots on the blue lines, making sure they stay within the frame, and in front of the blue lines: ctrl + click > Arrange > Bring to Front (⇧ + ⌘+]).

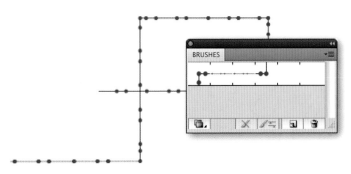

Curved corners tutorial

The second way to create perfectly aligned corners is a curved corner. While this tutorial may sound complicated, once you've mastered it, this method can be a great quick cheat.

Making the Stripes Pattern brush Side tile is easy; you just need five rectangles the same length, evenly spaced, filled with a bright color. From this Side tile we can make the corners.

1.   Load the Side tile artwork into a new Pattern brush. There is no need for a frame.

2.   Use the Rounded Rectangle Tool (under the Rectangle Tool), to draw a rounded corner rectangle and apply the brush to it.

3.   Expand the rounded corner rectangle: Object > Expand Appearance, this will release the brush artwork into its separate elements. Ungroup all the elements: Object > Ungroup (⇧ + ⌘ + G).

4.   Remove all the elements, apart from the ones that make up the upper right-hand corner.

5.   Draw a square frame over the corner elements. Duplicate your new frame, by copying and pasting it in place (⌘ + C, ⌘ + F). Select the duplicate frame along with the corner artwork elements and use the Pathfinders: Divide effect, and then ungroup.

6.   Remove all the elements that fall outside of the frame.

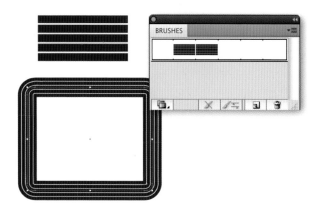

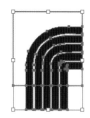

7. Adjust the size of the original frame so that the stripes sit in the middle of the frame's edges—this is essential if your corner tiles are to align with your Side tiles. You can calculate this however you like, but an easy way is to use the bottom edge as a guide: select the top left corner anchor point and use it to drag the frame smaller, while holding down ⇧ (shift), until both the right and left edges of the frame touch the stripes. Then select the top middle anchor point and drag the frame larger, while holding down ⇧ (shift), until the right-hand edge of the frame meets the right-hand edge of the stripes.

8. Make sure that the right-hand and bottom edges are sitting flush with the edges of your frame, using the align buttons.

9. Now load your new Corner tile into your existing stripes brush, making sure to import the frame as well as the artwork. In this instance, you can use the same artwork for both the Outer and Inner Corner tiles.

10. When you paint with the stripes brush, even on a square cornered path, you should get accurately aligned curved corners. If your tiles don't align, it will be because the stripes are not in the middle of the frame edges.

Curved corner frame rules:
- The corner frame must be square
- The edge of the design (x) must sit in the middle of the edge of the tile (y)
- The artwork must be flush with both the bottom and right edge of the square frame.

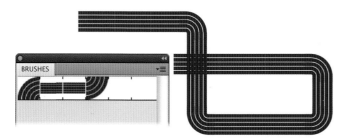

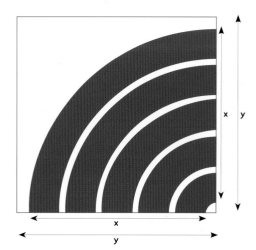

Corners only tutorial

Although all Pattern brushes must include and must start with a Side tile, it doesn't necessarily mean they have to be seen.

In the case of a brush like Photo Corners 1 (see page 210), the corner tiles are only tiles you see when the brush is applied to a path. To make this possible, you have to create an invisible Side tile.

1. Make your Corner tile designs, and group all the elements together within each design: Object > Group (⌘ + G).

2. Making an invisible Side tile is as easy as drawing a box with no stroke or fill color and loading it into a Pattern brush, then you can add the corner tiles to your new brush.

3. If, however, you want your corner tiles to sit in a certain position when placed on a path, it is necessary to add empty space to your corner tiles. It is always the center of the corner tile that is positioned on a path. Which, in the case of Photo Corners 1, means they sit away from the path, and not slightly overlapping it—which is the effect you want.

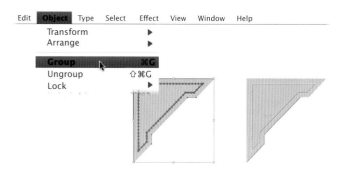

Corner tile brush applied to path with no white space added

4. Draw a frame with no stroke or fill color over one of your corner tiles, making sure it sits flush with the bottom and right-hand edges of the tile artwork.

5. Size the frame so that its center is roughly in the center of your corner tile design. It is not necessary to be exact about the size of positioning of your frame, because there are no visible Side tiles to align with.

6. Move the frame behind the tile design: ctrl + click > Arrange > Send to Back (⇧ + ⌘+ [). The empty frame will only register as part of the brush when sat behind the artwork.

7. Repeat steps 4 and 5 for your other corner tile.

8. Now import the two corner tile designs (including their empty frames) into the brush you created with the empty Side tile. This adapted brush's corner tiles should slightly overlap the path they sit on—perfect for framing pictures.

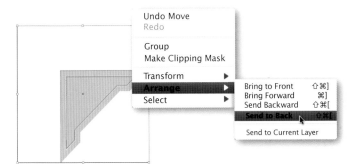

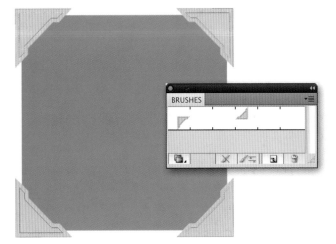

What can't be a brush?

Calligraphic brushes can only be ellipses, so they are a different matter altogether, but Scatter, Art, and Pattern brushes can be made from pretty much any vector illustration. However, there are certain illustration elements that can't be in a brush:

- gradients
- drop shadows
- other brush strokes
- imported images
- bitmap images
- clipping masks
- type (this only applies to Art and Pattern brushes, type **can** be used in Scatter brushes)
- graphs
- mesh objects

However, there are certain ways around some of these limitations:

Gradients can be expanded, or achieved with an Object Blend (see pages 229 to 235).

Drop shadows can be falsified using Object Blend (see pages 236 to 237).

Other brush strokes can be used, but they must be expanded (Object > Expand Appearance) before you try to make a new brush from them.

Imported or bitmap images can be replicated with Live Trace. You won't necessarily manage to recreate them exactly, but you can get pretty close (see pages 238 to 245).

Clipping masks can be replaced with the Pathfinder Shape Modes: Intersect Shape Area function. This does mean you'll permanently crop your image, but it may be worth it to achieve your desired effect. To use the Intersect Shape Area function, you must first remove the clipping path and ungroup the objects. Make sure that the image you're trying to crop is one image, and not a group of images, and that the frame you want to crop your image to is positioned in front.

Type can be used in an Art or Pattern brush if you outline it first. Using type in an Art brush can be a great way of distorting characters.

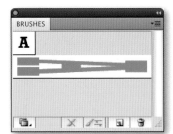

Gradients

You can't make a brush out of an illustration that contains a gradient, it will be rejected. Which is a shame because gradients can add sophistication or softness to a potential brush. But all is not lost as there are two ways around this problem: Expand gradient and Object Blend. Both these solutions give the same result—a series of colored bands, which gradually shift from one color to another.

Expand Gradient

Creating an expanded gradient is simple. Once you've colored an object with a gradient, go to Object > Expand... Make sure the gradiented area of your object is checked, be it Fill or Stroke, and Expand Gradient To is on Specify Objects, rather than Gradient Mesh. Then click OK.

This turns the gradient into a series of slices of different colors, and each slice is its own object (although they are all grouped). You can determine how many slices your gradient is chopped into by changing the number in the Expand Gradient To > Specify box.

If your object is anything other than a simple square or rectangle, you'll see that your expanded bands of color are in a clipping path, and illustrations that contain clipping paths can't be made into brushes either. So it's necessary to trim the bands to your shape by using the Pathfinders feature Select Divide.

Now you have an object with the appearance of a gradient that can be made into a brush.

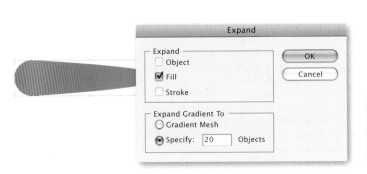

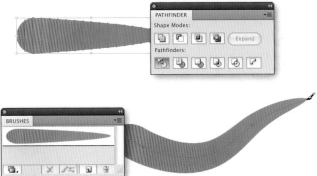

Object Blend

An Object Blend isn't primarily designed to produce a gradient effect. What it does is create a series of intermediate objects and colors, between two or more selected objects. But, if these original objects are close enough (or overlapping) and there are enough intermediate objects placed between them, then the result is a gradient look.

Once you've drawn your two or more objects, given them different colors, and selected them, there are three ways to make an Object Blend:

1. With the Blend tool (the icon of a square turning into a circle).

2. Object > Blend > Make.

3. The shortcut: alt + apple + B.

Once you've blended your objects, you will see the original objects and a path joining them (this path is called a spine), but you won't see all the bounding boxes for the new objects placed between. Your blended objects can make a brush as they are, because unlike gradients or clipping paths, blends can be used in brushes. However, if you wanted to get the bounding boxes for all the shapes in between, you need to go to Object > Expand... or Object > Blend > Expand.

1.

2.

Spines

When you make a blend, the spine created between the original objects will automatically be straight, but you can shape your spine before or after you make your blend.

Before you make your blend, you can draw the spine you want the blend to follow. Draw a Path that starts over your first object and ends on your last, making sure the path doesn't have any fill or stroke color. Select all the objects and your drawn path, then go to Object > Blend > Make. You'll see the blend follows your path.

If your blend is already made, you can still adjust the spine. A spine is essentially a path, so can be adjusted with anchor points and handles—you can add points, remove points, move them, and curve them. The blend will follow the changes you make to the spine.

You can also replace a spine altogether. Draw a new path starting over one object and ending on the other; again, be sure that your new spine doesn't have any fill or stroke color. Then select both your new path and your existing blend and go to Object > Blend > Replace Spine.

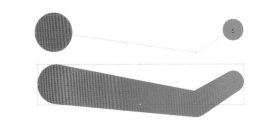

Draw spine

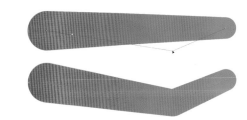

Edit spine

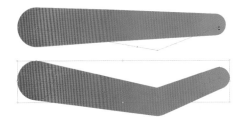

Replace spine

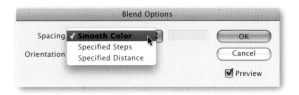

Blend options

There are options within the Blend function. These can be accessed from the Blend menu: Object > Blend > Blend Options… or by double-clicking the Blend Tool icon.

There are three modes of Blend: Smooth Color, Specified Steps, and Specified Distance.

Smooth Color is the default mode. This automatically calculates the optimum number of objects to place to create a smooth color transition.

Specified Steps lets you determine the number of objects to be placed.

Specified Distance lets you determine the distance between each object placed.

There are also Orientation Options, which only take effect if your two original objects are not overlapping and you have a curved spine to your blend.

You can choose between Align to Page and Align to Path. You can see the difference between the two settings most clearly when the objects placed in between are clearly separated.

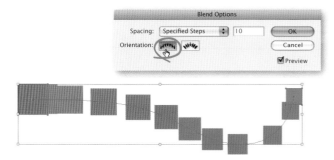

Align to Page means that all the objects placed in between will not rotate, but will all keep the orientation of the original objects.

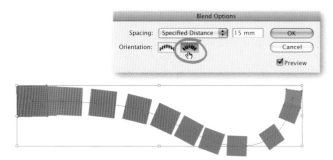

Align to Path means that all the objects placed in between will rotate to the curve of the spine.

Blend tool

To use the Blend tool, just click on your first object, then on your second, then onto the next, etc. The Blend tool gives you more control over your blend than the menu Blend command.

With the Blend tool you can determine the start and end point of your blend. If you click the Blend Tool in the middle of your objects, you get a blend as you would by using the menu Blend command. But, if you click the Blend tool on the anchor points of your shape (you'll notice the square goes from white to black), your blend will form from point to point.

Blended from the middle to middle

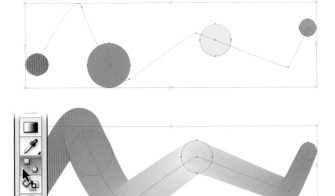

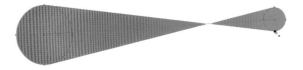

Blended from the top anchor point to bottom anchor point

Gradient tutorial

The following tutorial illustrates how to employ these gradient tricks in the creation of the Stack of Coins Scatter brush.

1. How can you create a brush which appears to be a stack of gold coins? Start by drawing one coin, which will be repeated to make your stack. Your original coin must be a straight-on side view, with flat top and bottom edges, so that it can meet flush with the coins above and below it when on a path.

2. To transform this flat rectangle into a curved coin, color it with a gradient going from dark gold at the edges to light gold in the middle

3. Now expand the gradient Object > Expand... Make sure Fill is checked, and Expand Gradient To is on Specify Objects, rather than Gradient Mesh. Then click OK.

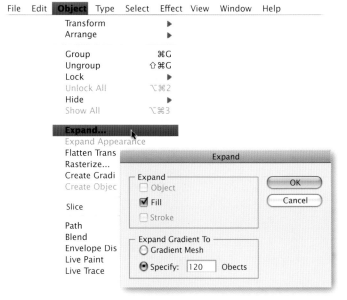

4. To create a series of grooves in the side profile of your coin, draw three narrow rectangles over your coin (each with the same height): one at the left edge, one in the center, and one on the right edge. The outer rectangles should be narrower than the center one.

5. Color the outer rectangles in a darker gold and the center one in a lighter shade.

6. Open the Blend Option window (Object > Blend > Blend Options... or double-click the Blend Tool icon), and change Spacing to 15 Specified Steps, and make sure that the rotation is Align to Page.

7. Choose the Blend tool, click on the center of your left-hand rectangle, then in the center of your middle rectangle, and finally, in the center of your right-hand rectangle. You should get a series of 30 rectangles that gradually change from thin, dark gold to thicker, light gold, then back to thin, dark gold.

8. Now you have an illustration ready to be imported as a Scatter brush.

9. When setting your Scatter Brush Options, make sure there is no space between your coins when they sit on a vertical path. To do this you'll need to set the Spacing somewhere below 100% depending on the size of your coin. Having a test stroke and preview check in your Scatter Brush Options window will help.

10. Put a slight random Scatter on your brush to make the coins pile up unevenly.

11. When you're happy with your Options settings, click OK, and you're ready to create great piles of gold!

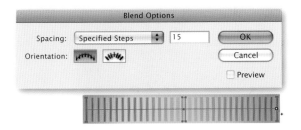

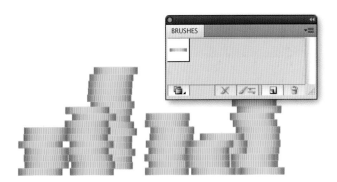

Drop Shadow tutorial

On some occasions you may want your brush to have a semitransparent shadow, so the object is opaque and the shadow can overlay in a realistic manner. The good news is that transparencies can be used in brushes, the bad news is that Drop Shadows can't. But, as usual, there is a way around this. With the help of an Object Blend, you can cheat your way to a realistic shadow.

The Scatter brush Chocolate Candies (see page 79), is a prime example of a design where a semitransparent shadow adds great depth.

1. Draw the shape you want your shadow to be. In the case of the Chocolate Candies, this is a simple oval.

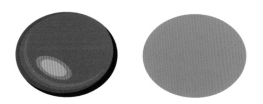

2. Select your shadow shape, and go to Object > Path > Offset Path... Enter a minus number into the Offset box—the number you need will depend on the size of your original object. Use the Preview function to judge what value is right for your image, and then click OK.

3. Color the outer shape in white and the inner shape in a dark gray.

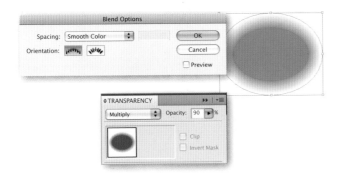

7. Now create your brush as normal.

8. When setting your Scatter Brush Options, experiment with close spacing, so that your candies overlap and cast a shadow onto one another.

4. Select both shapes and blend them together: go to Object > Blend > Make (alt + ⌘ + B), or use the Blend tool. For this blend you can leave the Object Blend Spacing on Smooth Color—the default setting.

5. Set the Transparency to Multiply and the Opacity to 90%.

6. Position the shadow behind your candy illustration (⇧ + ⌘ + [) and slightly off center, making sure that the solid dark gray center is hidden behind the candy.

Live Trace

Although imported or bitmap images can't be used in the creation of a brush, they can be turned into a vector image using Live Trace, and then used as a brush. You can Live Trace Bitmap, TIFF, JPEG, PNG, GIF, and PSD Files.

Live Trace can't reproduce your image exactly, but with the right settings it can closely match the lines and shapes, or it can create a far more abstract version of the image, which is sometimes more interesting. The crisper and larger the original image, the more accurate your trace will be.

In order to get from a bitmap image to a completely editable vector image, Live Trace works in two stages. First Live Trace your image and then Expand it. Only once you've expanded your image will each of the objects in your traced image be given their own path and bounding box. However, an image which has been traced, but not yet expanded, can still be a brush.

To Live Trace an image, first you must select it and then click on the Live Trace button found in the Control panel, or choose Object > Live Trace > Make.

Original Image

Live-traced images with different options

Live Trace options

As with most Illustrator features, Live Trace has a number of highly adjustable settings, all of which can be found in the Tracing Options window. These options can be adjusted before or after you've traced your image, and as many times as you like. You only finalize the visual when you click Expand.

Live Trace options

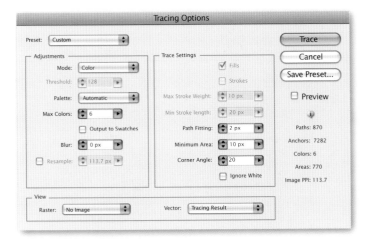

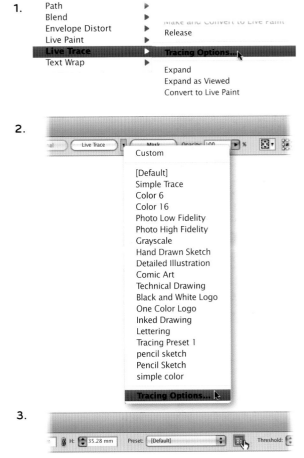

There are three ways to open the Tracing Options window:

1. Go to Object > Live Trace > Tracing Options (before and after you've traced your object)

2. Press the downwards arrow next to the Live Trace button, and scroll down to Tracing Options... (only before you've traced your object)

3. Press the Tracing Options button in the control panel (only after you've traced your object)

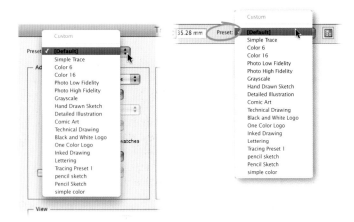

Preset is a drop-down menu with a number of built-in presets to achieve different looks. You can add your own presets by adjusting the various options, and then clicking the Save Preset button. This same list can also be accessed from the downward arrow next to the Live Trace button before you've traced your object.

Adjustments:
- **Mode** is the color mode which your image will be traced in: Color, Grayscale, or Black and White.

- **Threshold** works with the Black and White mode, and sets the black versus white ratio when tracing. The higher the threshold value, the more black there will be in the traced image. This tracing option is also available directly from the control panel.

- **Palette** works with the Color and Grayscale modes and sets the colors that will be in your traced image. The default setting for Palette is Automatic, which means Illustrator chooses the colors based on the colors it finds in your original image. If you want to specify a palette, then you must first open a color palette in your Illustrator document. You can either choose one of the built-in Illustrator color palettes or create your own—select the color you want to be in the palette then go to swatches: Menu > Save Swatch Library as…. As long as you have a Swatch Libary open before you open your Tracing Option window, then you will find the name of the palette in the drop-down palette menu.

- **Max Colors** works with the Color and Grayscale modes and specifies a maximum number of colors which will be used in your traced image.

- **Output To Swatches** creates a new swatch in the Swatches panel for each color in the tracing result.

- **Blur** sets the level of blurring which is applied during the trace. Blur can be useful for smoothing an image if your original image is particularly low resolution or has very rough edges.

- **Resample** changes the resolution of your original image before tracing it. This setting can be very useful if you are trying to trace a particularly large image, which would take a long time and produce a complicated image if you didn't resample it.

Trace Settings:

- **Fills** only works with the Black and White mode, and when checked, will produce a traced image with filled shapes.

- **Strokes** only works with the Black and White mode, and when checked creates stroked open paths for all objects that fall within the Max Stroke Weight setting—any object that is larger than the Max Stroke Weight will be an unfilled object, outlined with a 1pt stroke. Live Trace can apply different stroke widths to each path, which you can set with the Max Stroke Weight and the Min Stroke Length settings.

- **Max Stroke Weight** sets the maximum width of a stroke that will be applied in the traced image.

- **Min Stroke Length** sets the shortest path which will be in the traced image.

- **Path Fitting** controls how closely the lines of your traced image follow the original pixel image. The lower the Path Fitting value, the closer the traced image will be to the original image.

- **Minimum Area** specifies the smallest feature in the original image that will be traced. The lower the Minimum Area value, the more detail your traced image will contain. This tracing option is also available directly from the control panel.

- **Corner Angle** determines how acute an angle should be in your original pixel image for it to be a corner anchor point in your traced image. The lower the Corner Angle value, the more corners and sharp angles you will have in your traced image.

- **Ignore White** means that, when checked, any area of white in your original image will not be traced; instead, there will be an empty space with no path, stroke, or fill. This function can be useful if you have a clearly defined image on a white background, and you want to get rid of the background.

View: These options determine what you will see when using the preview feature and what you will see once you press Trace. These settings can't be saved as part of the tracing preset.

- **Raster** specifies how to display your original pixel image. This same menu of options can also be accessed from the button on the control panel.

- **Vector** specifies how to display your traced image. This same menu of options can also be accessed from the button on the control panel.

Preview will show you how your settings will affect your image, and having it selected while adjusting your settings can be the easiest way to be sure your settings will produce the result you're looking for.

i is a list of statistics which your current settings would produce in your traced image. It features paths, anchors, colors, areas, and image PPI.

Raster button in control panel

Vector button in control panel

Live Trace tutorial

A hand-drawn illustration scanned into the computer cannot be used as part of a brush in its bitmap form, but if you Live Trace it on the right settings, then not only can you maintain that hand-drawn look, you can also make it into a brush. This means you can produce a large illustration very quickly that looks like it has taken hours to hand render.

1. Draw a simple flower with stem, making sure the stem is reasonably straight.

2. The drawing can be as rough as you like, but try to erase any lines you don't want to be in your final brush, or do your underdrawing in one color and draw the final image over the top in another—this will help Live Trace distinguish between the line you want and the ones you don't.

3. Scan in your image and open or place the file into an Illustrator document. You can do this by opening an image file from within Illustrator: File > Open, or placing an image: File > Place.

4. Select your image and go to Object > Live Trace > Tracing Options.

5. You may get a warning window come up, telling you that your image is large and that the trace will be slow. Click OK. When the Tracing Option window appears, Resample your illustration to around 150 px, this will speed up the tracing.

6. Make sure you have Preview checked, so that the effect of your setting can be viewed on your illustration. You'll see that your image has been transformed into a simple black and white illustration—the default preset.

7. You want your illustration to be black and white, so that when you set your brush Colorization method to Tints, your brush strokes will be 100% the stroke color in your color palette. So leave the Mode, but you may have to adjust your Threshold slider, to bring out the detail.

8. You can either leave your illustration very rough and sketchy or you can adjust the Blur and Resample settings to get a smoother look. Often, if you resample you image to a low figure, it will have the same effect as adding blur.

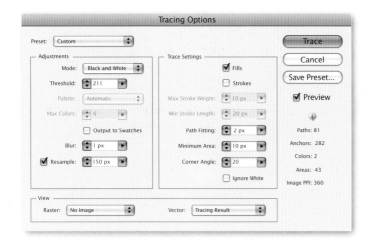

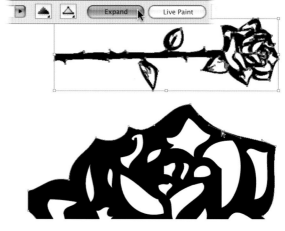

9. When you are happy with the level of detail and smoothness, click Trace.

10. The Tracing Options box will close, and you'll have your traced image in place of your pixel image. Your image still only has one bounding box, and it hasn't been split into individual elements—this is because it hasn't yet been expanded. At this stage you can still call up the Tracing Options window again and adjust the settings.

11. When you are completely happy with the settings, press Expand, and the artwork will be divided into all its separate elements.

12. Ungroup the elements: Object > Ungroup (⇧ + ⌘ + G).

13. Select and remove the background and make any final tweaks to your flower. When you are adjusting anchor points, remember that you want the white and black shapes to match up, so there are no holes in your brush.

14. Select and group all the elements: Object > Group (⌘ + G).

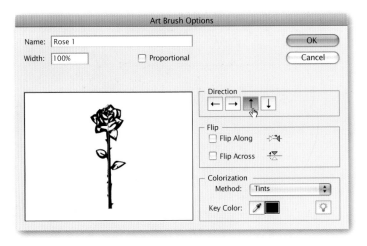

Art Brush Options

Name: Rose 1

Width: 100%   ☐ Proportional

OK

Cancel

Direction
← → ↑ ↓

Flip
☐ Flip Along
☐ Flip Across

Colorization
Method: Tints
Key Color: ▰ ■   ♡

17. Change the Colorization method to Tints, so that what is currently black in the brush will be whatever stroke color you paint with, and the white in the brush will stay white.

18. Name your brush and click OK.

19. Change the stroke color as you paint, and you can create a bunch of hand-drawn flowers in seconds.

15. You're now ready for your flower to become an Art brush. Art brushes are perfect for natural objects because you can bend them on a curved path.

16. In your Art Brush Options window make sure the direction is going from the stem base to the flower head.

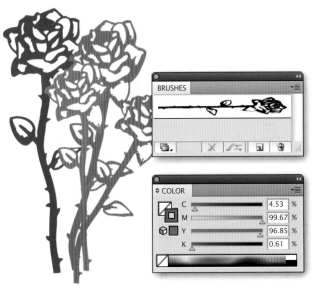

BRUSHES

⊟ | ✕ | ⚏ | ▣ | 🗑

COLOR

C ▱ — 4.53 %
M ▱ — 99.67 %
Y ▱ — 96.85 %
K ▱ — 0.61 %

Adapting an existing brush

You can edit the way an existing brush applies to a path by editing its options, but you can also edit the original artwork of an existing Scatter, Art, or Pattern brush.

1. Drag an existing brush out of the Brushes palette onto your art board.

2. The brush artwork will be grouped together with a rectangular frame. Select the artwork and go to: Object > Ungroup (⇧ + ⌘ + G).

3. Remove the rectangular frame, and edit any aspects of the brush you choose.

4. Once you're happy with your revised brush artwork, group all the elements back together: Object > Group (⌘ + G).

5. Now you can either make a new Art brush, or you can replace the existing brush by dragging your new artwork over the existing brush in the Brushes palette while holding down alt.

6. If you decide to replace an existing brush, the option window for that brush will open. If that existing brush was already applied to a path in your document, when you press OK another window will appear asking if you want to apply the changes to the existing brush strokes. If you click Apply to Strokes, the existing stroke will change. If you click Leave Strokes, your adapted brush will become an entirely new brush, leaving the old brush in your Brushes palette—this is another way of taking the setting from the existing brush without replacing it.

Tip:
If you are adapting a Pattern brush, you can replace individual tiles by dragging new tile artwork over the existing tile in the Brushes palette, while holding down alt.

Transparency

The Transparency settings can be applied to a brush in two ways: through the original illustration that you make your brush from, or the path that you apply a brush to.

Original illustration transparency

All the Transparency settings can be used in the creation of a Scatter, Art, or Pattern brush. Calligraphic brushes don't start with an original illustration, so can't have Transparency settings added at this stage.

Any Scatter, Art, or Pattern brush that is created with a transparent illustration will be transparent against a background and over any strokes they cross. But in a single stroke, Scatter and Pattern brushes will also appear transparent when they overlap themselves.

Path transparency

Path transparency can be added to any brush type, including Calligraphic brush strokes. The difference between when you make the path transparent, rather than the original illustration, is that single strokes of Scatter or Pattern brushes will not be transparent when they overlap themselves. They will only be transparent over a background or other strokes.

Transparency blends

The Transparency settings can also be used in conjunction with an Object Blend to make an object that graduates from opaque to transparent.

For example, make two circles, one with no transparency settings and the other set to 50% Opacity. Set them apart. Select both circles and go to Object > Blend > Make, or press alt + apple + B. Then load this illustration into your Brushes palette as a new Art brush. The result is a brush that gradually goes from 100% to 50% opacity. Because it's an Art brush, you won't see the transparency when a single stroke overlaps itself, but you will see it on a background and when separate strokes overlap. This method of transparency blending can also be used on Scatter and Pattern brushes.

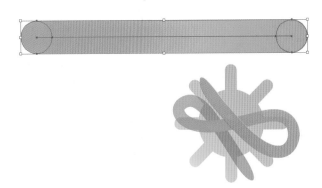

Lines or outlines

When a brush is applied to a path, you can edit the anchor points of the path, but not of the brush illustration. To do this you must either paint with the Blob Brush (which limits you to Calligraphic brushes only), or you must expand your brush strokes.

To expand a brush stroke, select the path with the brush applied to it and go to Object > Expand Appearance or Object > Path > Outline Stroke.

Expanding a brush stroke converts it back to an object, with its own path, anchor points, and bounding box. If the brush has a number of elements, these will become separate objects, as they were in the original illustration that made the brush, but they will be grouped together. To ungroup them, go to Object > Ungroup (⇧ + ⌘ + G).

Once you have expanded a brush stroke, it is no longer controlled by the path it was on. The path will still be there, but if you edit it the brush illustration will not follow. So it is important that you are 100% happy with the shape of your path, before you expand it.

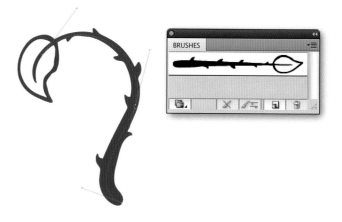

Keyboard shortcuts for Illustrator CS4

Illustrator is awash with keyboard shortcuts, which can really speed up your work. This is by no means the entire list, but a selection that can be handy when working with brushes. (Although these shortcuts are specifically for CS4, the majority are the same for previous versions of Illustrator.)

Mac keyboard shortcut tips

Modifier keys on Apple Mac computers are sometimes referred to by their names and sometimes their symbols. For the purpose of this book, they are labels by the symbols which appear on the keys. For reference, here are the names the keys are given in some other texts:

⌘ = Command   ctrl (or ^)= Control
⇧ = Shift   ⇪ = Caps Lock
alt (or ⌥) = alt or Option

Tools	Mac	Windows
Selection	V	V
Direct Selection	A	A
Magic Wand	Y	Y
Lasso	Q	Q
Paintbrush	B	B
Blob Brush	⇧ + B	Shift + B
Pen	P	P
Pencil	N	N
Rotate	R	R
Reflect	O	O
Scale	S	S
Warp	⇧ + R	Shift + R

Free Transform	E	E
Slice	⇧ + K	Shift + K
Erase	⇧ + E	Shift + E
Scissors	C	C
Eyedropper	I	I
Zoom	Z	Z
Add Anchor Point	+	+
Delete Anchor Point	-	-
Convert Anchor Point	⇧ + C	Shift + C
Show Tools options	Double-click on tool icon	Double-click on tool icon
Change tool pointer to cross hair	⇪	Caps Lock

Keyboard shortcuts for Illustrator CS4

Drawing and editing	Mac	Windows
Create and expand a Live Trace object in one step	alt click Live Trace in the Control panel	Alt click Live Trace in the Control panel
Increase size of Blob Brush	]	]
Decrease size of Blob Brush	[	[
Constrain Blob Brush path horizontally or vertically	⇧	Shift
Move a shape while drawing it	Spacebar + drag	Spacebar + drag
Constrain movement to 45°, 90°, 135°, or 180°	Hold down ⇧	Hold down Shift
Constrain proportions or orientation	Hold down ⇧	Hold down Shift
Switch Pen tool to Convert Anchor Point tool	alt	Alt
Switch between Add Anchor Point tool and Delete Anchor Point tool	alt	Alt
Move current anchor point while drawing with Pen tool	Spacebar + Drag	Spacebar + Drag
Cut a straight line with Knife tool	alt + drag	Alt + drag
Cut a 45° or 90° line with Knife tool	⇧ + alt + drag	Shift + Alt + drag

	Mac	Windows
Toggle between fill and stroke	X	X
Set fill and stroke to default	D	D
Swap fill and stroke	⇧ + X	Shift + X
Select color fill mode	<	<
Select no stroke/fill mode	/	/
Switch to last used selection tool	ctrl	Ctrl
Duplicate selection	alt + drag	Alt + drag
Duplicate selection and keep it horizontally or vertically parallel	⇧ + alt + drag	Shift + Alt + drag
Scale proportionally with Selection Tool	⇧ + drag bounding box	Shift + drag bounding box
Scale from center with Selection tool	alt + drag bounding box	Alt + drag bounding box
Create closed path with Pen, pencil, Paintbrush, or Blob Brush tools	Hold down alt + release mouse/pen	Hold down Alt + release mouse/pen

Viewing artwork	Mac	Windows
Toggle between screen modes	F	F
Fit imagable area in window	Double click on Hand tool	Double click on Hand tool
Switch to Hand tool	⌘ + O	Spacebar
Zoom In tool	Z	Ctrl + Spacebar
Show/Hide artboards	⌘ + ⇧ + H	Ctrl + Shift + H
Show/Hide artboard rulers	⌘ + alt + R	Ctrl + Alt + R
View all artboards in window	⌘ + alt + 0	Ctrl + Alt + 0
Exit Artboard tool mode	Esc	Esc
Navigate to next document	⌘ + `	Ctrl + F6
Navigate to previous document	⌘ + ⇧ + `	Ctrl + Alt + F6
Save multiple artboards to CS3 or earlier version	alt + v	Alt + V
Outline Mode	⌘ + Y	Ctrl + Y

Panels	Mac	Windows
Show/hide brushes	F5	F5
Open brush options window	Double click on brush	Double click on brush
Duplicate brush	Drag brush to New Brush icon	Drag brush to New Brush icon
Show/hide color	F6	F6
Show/hide layers	F7	F7
Show/hide info	⌘ + F8	Ctrl + F8
Show/hide gradient	⌘ + F9	Ctrl + F9
Show/hide strokes	⌘ + F10	Ctrl + F10
Show/hide attributes	⌘ + F11	Ctrl + F11
Show/hide graphic styles	⇧ + F5	Shift + F5
Show/hide appearance	⇧ + F6	Shift + F6
Show/hide align	⇧ + F7	Shift + F7
Show/hide transform	⇧ + F8	Shift + F8
Show/hide pathfinder	⇧ + ⌘ + F9	Shift + Ctrl + F9
Show/hide transparency	⇧ + ⌘ + F10	Shift + Ctrl + F10

Powerball by André SMATIK Ljosaj

Contact details

Adam Lewis
adamjon1@hotmail.com

André Nossek
www.vgrfk.com / info@vgrfk.com

André SMATIK Ljosaj
www.smatik.de / info@smatik.de

Ben the Illustrator
www.bentheillustrator.com / hello@bentheillustrator.com

Cengiz Bodur
www.tasarix.com / contact@tasarix.com

David Caunce
www.imagine-cga.co.uk / info@imagine-cga.co.uk

Emily Portnoi
emilyillustration@googlemail.com

hellron
hellron.deviantart.com / enron@hotmail.com

Ilias Sounas
www.sounasdesign.com / sounas@gmail.com

Julian James
whyisbox.com / hello@whyisbox.com

Leo Volland
www.vgrfk.com / info@vgrfk.com

Saurabh Gupta
saurabh_gupta@hotmail.com

Weirdink
www.weirdink.com / weirdink@gamil.com

Josh Scruggs
www.26symbols.com / josh@scruggsdesign.com

Index

Acknowledgments

Thanks to everyone at RotoVision for their support and encouragement, especially April Sankey and Tony Seddon for thinking this book might be a good idea.

Special thanks to:

Luke Herriott for all his time and effort gathering the work featured in this book.

All the talented people who kindly contributed their work.

Jane Roe for being a wonderful editor and always coloring in my o's.

Lisa Båtsvik-Miller for keeping me company on the many late nights spent creating brushes.

And finally, my fiancé Jeremy, for all the washing-up.

GAYLORD